# A DROP IN THE OCEAN OF LOVE:

# ANCIENT WISDOM FOR LIVING A DIVINELY-GUIDED LIFE

# A Drop in the Ocean of Love

## Ancient Wisdom for Living a Divinely-Guided Life

Presented by

**The University of Spiritual Healing and Sufism**

www.SufiUniversity.org

For more information, contact:
The University of Spiritual Healing and Sufism
P.O. Box 729, Angwin, CA 94508
www.SufiUniversity.org

Publisher: DPWN Publishing
1879 N. Neltnor Blvd. #316, West Chicago, IL 60185
www.DPWN Publishing.com

Printed in the United States of America

ISBN: 978-1-939794-10-9

# In the Name of the One.

Anything of truth written here has come from the One.
Any mistakes or omissions are from ourselves.

# Dedication

To our spiritual guide, Sidi Shaykh Muhammad al-Jamal, guide of the
Shadhiliyya Sufi Order and Head of the Higher Sufi Council in Jerusalem
and the Holy Land.

Sidi lived as a true servant of God, spreading the message of peace, love,
mercy, justice and freedom to the world. We are honored and blessed to have
been transformed through his service, by the Grace of Allah.

With love and gratitude for all you have given to us. May Allah continue to
guide us in the mission He brought to us through your loving presence.

To the many others not included in this book who have answered the call
to dive into the Ocean of Divine Love and follow this path of deep healing,
reverence for God and Divinely-guided service to the world.

To all who have been called in spirit, who are seeking the guidance and
support to walk along the shore, to wade into the surf or to dive into the
depths of exquisite beauty.

To all of you who are yet to come. To you who yearn to truly know
yourselves; to know God through your own hearts; to swim in the depths of
the ocean, as drops realizing that they have never been separate, but that they
are and always have been one with The Ocean of Love.

# Introduction

A Sufi guide knows his students from before they were born. There is a pre-destined Divine orchestration that brings us together in this life to follow a common path and to serve a common purpose.

Each of the authors of this book was called to be a student of Sidi Shaykh Muhammad al-Jamal, the guide of the Shadhiliyya Sufi Order and Head of the Higher Sufi Council in Jerusalem and the Holy Land.

In the beginning, none could have imagined what would lie ahead on this path. It is like discovering an exquisite ocean of Divine love and beauty, diving in, and then discovering that the ocean you're swimming in is alive in your own heart.

All human beings are born with the knowing of the Essence of God in their hearts. The ocean of Divine Essence is contained within every drop of the Creation. However, even the ocean experiences storms. Life happens, and the essence within gets covered over with layers of protection. Before we realize the nature of the ocean we live in, we spend a lot of time putting on wet suits, building life rafts, dropping anchors and tying ourselves to piers to create safety for ourselves and our loved ones.

We form beliefs about what we need to do or be in order to survive and be successful in this physical world. We become confused and temporarily lose our way.

However, we are not lost. We are learning every step of the way. We are always between the hands of the Beloved. The drop in the Ocean is never separate from the Ocean Itself.

Then one day we realize that the limitations we've created are too constraining, and we long to break free to find a life of depth, purpose and freedom.

The poet Jalal id-din Rumi said,

*"Your path is not to seek for love,*
*but merely to seek and find all the barriers you have built against it."*

Sufism is about purification of the heart. The path we follow is about washing away the barriers that veil the heart, so we can discover, release and live the truth that lies within.

The Sufi path is a path of Divine Love, which must be tasted to be truly understood. This is an ever-present state of being, which is different from the human emotion of love that ebbs and flows.

The only way to know honey is to taste it for yourself. We offer you these modern-day stories from our lives that have helped us to discover the sweetness of life.

These are stories of personal experiences and teachings that have purified our hearts and expanded our understandings of the meaning and purpose of life on this earth, and in the life that extends beyond this material existence.

Our hope is that by sharing our stories with you, you may find some reflection of yourself and travel with us through the beauty of your heart to discover the truth within you, to find the Divine Ocean that holds the secrets to living your life of peace, love, mercy, justice and freedom.

We invite you to dive into this book and taste the sweetness. Let it fill you, feed you and nourish your heart and soul. We pray that you find something of value here and discover hidden treasures for living your Divinely-guided life.

# Table of Contents

# *The Love*

# Kamila Carolyn Shenmen Ph.D., Dipl. Ac., Dipl.C.H., M.Div.

*Bismi'llah ir-rahman ir-rahim. In the Name of God, the Merciful, the Compassionate.*

"When you find the love, you find yourself. The secret is in the love. You are the love, not another."

"When God made you, He made beauty." — *Shaykh Muhammad Sa'id al-Jamal ar-Rifa'i ash-Shadhuli, (1).*

These words were not true for me as a small child growing up in a tiny mining town in the outback of Australia. I was the baby of the family, the youngest of three children, born two years after the end of the Second World War. As a result, mine was the only early childhood for which my father was present and I inherited the family role of "most loved, spoiled, youngest child." I was a very bright, active and strong-willed little girl, so I was also labelled "stubborn" and "bossy."

Despite my siblings' belief that I was the most loved child, that was not my experience. I have no recollection from childhood of ever hearing the words "I love you" from anyone. Of course, that was not the Aussie way in those days, but it is quite possible that those words were spoken to me at times and that I simply was not able to hear them. I remember myself as a small girl whose heart was full of love, looking for a place where that love would be welcomed and yearning for love in return. What made this impossible was that I knew that I was unlikeable and unlovable.

I don't know where this conviction that I was not likeable or lovable came from. It was simply there, present even in my earliest memories. It was a painful way to go through life, overflowing with love, trying desperately to feel loved by others and yet knowing that ultimately I was doomed to fail. In the Sufi tradition, we call these mistaken, yet firmly held, beliefs 'pictures' or 'voices.'

We human beings enter this world in a state of purity and wisdom, knowing the Unity from whence we come. Once here, we immediately begin to develop mistaken beliefs as a result of our experiences in the world. Something happens that leaves a strong impression on us, we form a faulty conclusion about what that experience means and that becomes our reality. For example, a baby cries and their mother does not respond immediately. Depending on the nature of the child, they may draw the conclusion that their mother does not love them or that the world is an unsafe, painful place. Another baby might create, instead, the picture that they have been abandoned.

The problem that these pictures create for us is that these mistaken beliefs become a window into the world through which we filter our life experiences. For me, very simply, every memorable event confirmed my lack of likeability or lovability. For example, being left out of an elementary school classmate's invitation to her birthday party left a painfully humiliating memory, while I have no recollection of the birthday parties that I *was* invited to during that time.

If something happened that appeared to contradict my belief, I simply didn't notice it or I found a way later to interpret the event so that it confirmed my belief. I remember that in high school I was elected head of my house (think Harry Potter!), when I had thought that one of my close friends was more popular than I and would thus be chosen. What stuck with me was the suggestion by another friend that the younger students had mixed up our names and so my election was a mistake. Likewise, when I was elected a school prefect in my senior year (Australian schools follow British traditions), I saw the list where my name was handwritten in third place. I concluded that the students hadn't really chosen me, but that a teacher had written my name in because of my stellar academic record.

When I graduated from high school, I won a scholarship to support me in attending university, and I chose to study Science, majoring in Molecular Biology and Genetics. I brought my lack of lovability with me, of course, that hadn't changed. What had changed was that I had learned to put a wall around my tender heart in an attempt to protect it from pain by keeping people out. What I didn't realize was that I had also walled myself off from my heart. Because the problem wasn't just that other people didn't like or love me, I didn't love myself either, and made every attempt to avoid being alone with my own being.

The years passed in this way. I married, studied, travelled, raised four wonderful children. God was very generous with me and it seemed that everything I asked for in this world, I received. I led an enviable life, by any standard, and yet I am aware that despite the charmed life I was leading in the outer world, there was always a place deep in my heart that was unhappy. Then at around the age of 40 my outer world began to fall apart. My marriage began to deteriorate and I developed serious health problems. My two older children became teenagers, began to manifest severe mood disorders and seemingly hated me! This was very bad news, because the only people I had allowed inside my wall were my husband and my children, and I had begun to hope that perhaps I was lovable after all. These new developments only served to reinforce my earlier picture, but with a new twist—people might love me at first, but once they really got to know me, they would stop!

I was in my early fifties when my eldest son introduced me to the Sufi tradition. He had found this spiritual path when seeking help for his depression and, knowing that I was also searching for a spiritual path, he introduced me to his teacher, Salima Adelstein, and his local Sufi group. I remember sitting in my first dhikr (remembrance) circle, hearing Salima say "Sufism is a path of the heart, a path of love" and feeling my heart immediately respond 'Yes, *this* is my spiritual path." Not long after I joined the Sufi community, Rahim Bronner, another teacher from the University of Spiritual Healing and Sufism (USHS) came into town to give a workshop. During the Friday evening introduction, Rahim talked about the Sufi path and the mistaken beliefs that come between us and our hearts' yearnings. He described the university's curriculum and led us in an experiential teaching to clear one of our pictures. Again, it was as if a light bulb lit up in my heart and I remember thinking "If that's what they're teaching at the university, *I'm going!*" I enrolled at USHS in the very next Fall class. I have been there ever since — first as a student, then as a teacher, and am forever grateful to Allah for leading me to the place that carried the medicine my heart needed.

Sufism and spiritual healing, and in particular the Shadhiliyya Sufi order, a healing order led by Shaykh Muhammad Sa'id al-Jamal ar-Rifa'i ash-Shadhuli, were not an obvious fit for me at the beginning. Sufism developed as the mystical inner dimension of Islam, which was a religion I had not even heard of growing up in the Australian outback. Sufism is a path of love, focused on the heart as our place of connection to the subtle Divine worlds, the locus of peace, love, higher wisdom and Divine healing. Meanwhile, I had spent a lifetime erecting a wall around my heart to keep people out, and by now, that included me! I had also spent my life immersed in science, and had believed for a long time that everything could ultimately be explained by science. So, I enrolled at The University of Spiritual Healing and Sufism, fully convinced that I had no subtle perception, could not feel my heart and would eventually be found to be incompetent by the faculty and flunk out in disgrace. But my desire for the healing I knew was there was so great that I took the leap anyway.

My first lengthy encounter with our Sufi Shaykh, affectionately known as Sidi, was initially a disappointment. I was attending a four-day event of classes, and sitting in front of the guide in the teaching tent for several days without feeling anything. Sure enough, I couldn't feel my heart, I hadn't immediately fallen in love with the Shaykh as some people reported and there were no signs of subtle perceptions of any kind. However, I was nothing if not desperate, so I continued to sit through his teachings nursing my defeat. On the very last teaching of the last day, as I quietly sat in front of him, I suddenly felt a loud "Ping!" in my upper chest and a large field of energy sprang to life around my heart. While I had been sitting there in my disappointment, my guide had been working in the inner worlds to reconnect me with my heart and to reopen my subtle perceptions. Since that day, I have never lost connection with my subtle heart. That connection is always there—the doorway to God's Love, Peace, Wisdom, Guidance and Oneness.

The mystical path of Sufism teaches us that the world was created by a Loving and Merciful God.

Our guide writes of Allah:

"Know My beloved, that I am a hidden treasure that longed to be known. So I have drawn forth all of the creation out of Myself in order to know Myself. But how can My creatures know Me? I planted all My qualities in the ground of creation. When any creature comes to know on what ground he stands, he discovers all My attributes in the ground of his existence. In the mirror of My attributes, he comes to see himself." (2)

The Qualities or Attributes of God are known by tradition in Sufism as the 99 Divine Names, and represent the infinite aspects of the Divine as He manifests Himself in Creation. Sufism also teaches us that the human being is the only being in creation who carries all of the Divine Names of God within his/her soul, and that the purified human heart is a mirror of the Divine. It is for this reason that many Sufi mystics have said "He who knows himself knows his Lord".

The pictures and voices of mistaken beliefs that we carry in this world serve to veil us from the beauty of the jewel we carry within our hearts. Each picture that we clear brings us one step closer to knowing the truth of who we are, experiencing the particular flavor of beauty that we carry and returning to that state of unity which is our birthright.

There are many practices taught by the Sufi masters that are designed to open our hearts to the Light of Allah, which bring Divine healing and purification. Many of these practices consist of the repetition of sacred phrases in the Arabic language, invoking the Beautiful Names of God, or invocations of the name "Allah," the Ocean of Love to which the streams of the Divine Names lead. These practices can be done alone or in a group. The Shadhiliyya Sufi order is a healing order, and at the University we teach many sacred healings, which have been transmitted by our guide. These healings come from a treasury of ancient prophetic knowledge, and are used to help others open their hearts to the healing Light of God.

As a student, I was very motivated. I loved being in class at USHS and I really wanted the healing that I sensed was available to me. I did all of the recommended practices, all of the assigned homework and I took every opportunity to give and receive spiritual healings with faculty, classmates, friends and family. I cannot say that there was ever an 'Aha' moment for me. There was no dramatic moment where everything changed and I don't remember ever receiving a healing where the focus was on my belief that I was unlovable. However, one day at some point during my journey on the Sufi path, I simply realized that this belief that I was not worthy of love was gone. With that simple realization, everything in my existence *has* changed. I now know that I am lovable, that I carry within me a kind, loving, compassionate heart that knows how to give and receive love. I also know that my heart is a manifestation of the Divine and that the love that flows through my heart to those around me is from Allah, not from my human self. And best of all, I know that the source of the Love I have sought my whole life is my Lord, and that this Love is available to me in every situation at every moment. This is the quality of al-Wadud, the Endlessly Loving, Whose love never fails and never changes.

The interesting thing is that once I was healed of this belief in my lack of lovability, everything around me also changed. Gone was the child who never heard the words "I love you." Suddenly, many people were telling me that they loved me—teachers, students, friends, family, my children. I was swimming in a sea of love!

One event that served to reinforce this new knowledge of my heart took place when I was in Vienna, in retreat, spending many hours a day in contemplation and remembrance of God. As I was sitting remembering Allah, my perception of the unseen world suddenly opened and I was given a glimpse of my own heart. I remember thinking "Oh, look at that. What a sweet heart that is!" It was over in a few moments, but it left a strong impression. Of course, I then tried to recreate the experience, and was unable to. I remember going to my teacher, Fawzia al-Rawi, telling her about it and saying that I hadn't been able to get that image back again. She wisely replied, "Well, don't try to get it back. Just remember it."

Another result of my access to the true source of the Love, is that I am less dependent on the love of other human beings. This has freed me to give love to people without being attached to whether I receive love in return. In this sense, all love is from Allah to Allah, and I am free of my old, painful need for human love. Of course, it is wonderful to be told that one is loved and I enjoy it very much. But I am also aware that it is Allah sending me love through another human being, and that ultimately it is Allah manifesting Love to Allah, in order to know Himself as the Love.

Many Sufi masters have expressed the opinion that all the 99 Divine Names are names of Love. We begin with the Name "Allah—the Eternal Reality, That Which Is". This is the first Name of Love. It is based on the Arabic verb *waliha*—meaning to love passionately, to love madly. Allah is the Name of the Essence (of God), which encompasses the presence of all the Names, indicating that all Divine Names are Names of Love. The 99 Names carry many different flavors of Love, some easy for us to recognize as love—Mercy, Compassion, Kindness, Tenderness, Gentleness, Subtle Love, Intimacy, Forgiveness, and some flavors that we humans find more difficult to understand as loving such as the Bringer of Death, the Avenger. Allah's manifestation is infinite and in perfect balance, between Beauty and Majesty. In order to know Himself completely, all aspects of the Divine are expressed. The more we come to know the Love of Allah, the more we recognize it within all the faces of God.

As I reflect on my life, I am filled with gratitude for Allah's blessings. No longer that young woman with a charmed life, carrying a kernel of sadness in my heart, I now find the reverse to be true. My outer life often looks difficult and painful, but when I connect into the deepest place in my heart, what I find there is peace, love and contentment. I am very thankful that my Lord chose to take me by the hand and guide me back to Him, the Source of All Goodness and Love. My wish for all human beings is the same—that we all truly know ourselves in order to know our Lord.

I end as I began, with a quote from our beloved guide, Sidi Muhammad al-Jamal.

"Know, my beloved, that the love is eternal between Allah and His creation and the electric circuitry of His love flows through everything. If not for this, nothing would move that moves; nothing would live that lives. Every planet in its orbit and every cell in its course is a witness to the love of Allah and a sign of His wisdom. Keep this love inside you and live with it all the time because the moment you lose it, you lose yourself; you lose Him. This is your message from your Beloved Allah, if you know Who speaks with you. I am the Love." (3)

Citations:

1. *Music of the Soul*, p.26. Shaykh Muhammad Sa'id al-Jamal ar-Rifa'i ash-Shadhuli

2. *Music of the Soul*, p.160. Shaykh Muhammad Sa'id al-Jamal ar-Rifa'i ash-Shadhuli

3. *Music of the Soul*, p.173. Shaykh Muhammad Sa'id al-Jamal ar-Rifa'i ash-Shadhuli

# Kamila Carolyn Shenmen Ph.D., Dipl.Ac., Dipl.C.H., M.Div.

Kamila Shenmen is Co-President, Dean of Faculty and Dean of Admissions of The University of Spiritual Healing & Sufism, as well as a graduate and faculty member.

Kamila holds a Doctorate in Computer Science and Molecular Biology and worked for 18 years at the National Institutes of Health in Bethesda, Maryland. She is a practitioner of Oriental Medicine, and a former faculty member and Clinic Director of the Maryland Institute of Traditional Chinese Medicine.

Kamila's search for healing at the deepest levels led her to study the ancient spiritual healing practices of Sufism with Shaykh Sidi Muhammad al-Jamal. Having found the peace and healing that comes from opening the heart to God's love, Kamila finds joy in sharing these teachings with her clients and students.

# *Love and Relationships: How Sidi's teachings have impacted my marriage and family, and my work with other families*

## Nura Laird, M.Ed.

"The power of love dominates. It crushes out caution and fear." (Dean Ornish, Commonweal Cancer Conference, Jan, 28, 2017)

I remember those days very clearly. It was in the spring of 1997 and we were at Salih Kent's house outside of Santa Fe, New Mexico. This is where he hosted Sidi for days or weeks. Sidi's longtime beloveds and others would come there to visit him and to receive his teachings. I was impressed by the loving atmosphere. Everyone shared the cooking for all the folks who came and went throughout the days of Sidi's visit there. There was an easy blending of seasoned students of Sidi with new people that included Muslims and non-Muslims, as well as adults and children.

At night, we all slept on the floor of Salih's living room, crowded like sardines, with Sidi sleeping right there among us. I'm a light sleeper, so throughout the night I could hear Sidi alternately snoring, chanting and calling out Allah or la ilaha ila llah in his sleep. There were late night trips to the bathroom, climbing over all the bodies in the dark. I especially remember when Sidi would make his way to the bathroom and stumble over us in the dark. I was always afraid that he would fall.

One day a woman, who had been Sidi's student for many years, came to Salih's with her 10-year-old son. The boy was large and bulky for his age.

As soon as he saw Sidi, who was teaching us while sitting cross-legged on a futon on the floor, the boy flung his large body across Sidi's lap. He lay on his back and proceeded to play with Sidi's beard and his kufia. He put Sidi's kufia on his own face and laughed. Sidi kept on teaching, unfazed. Eventually Sidi pointed down to the boy and spoke to us, "He is my very holy son who I love," and then resumed his teaching.

I was very moved by this scene. I love children and have long advocated for them to be loved and treated with respect and honor. That day I saw this holy man, whom I barely knew, treating that boy with love, respect and honor. The boy wasn't seen as rude or disrespectful. Instead, Sidi showered care upon him. It warmed my heart and immediately convinced me that Sidi was someone I could trust. This is because he understands us all, sees us deeply and honors and respects all of us, even the children. In that moment, I knew that I wanted to be the kind of person that he was. I didn't know about giving the promise (bayat) at that point, but I did make bayat with him two weeks later.

In the early 2000's, before Sidi began to live and teach at the Mother Center in California, he used to stay and teach nearby at the Lake House where we lived. He would stay there for days or weeks. He'd stay with us, cook with us, teach us and visit with us. Many people would come for a day, week, and even for several weeks.

Those of us who lived there were very busy taking care of the people, the house, and Sidi. It was more than a full-time job. Many days during that time, Wadude and I would rise early, go to bed late and barely have a chance to say a word to each other. One day, Sidi called us to him and spoke to us very deliberately with a concerned look in his eyes, "You must water your tree." We understood this to mean that it was important that we take care of our marriage, cultivate the love and even take time to make love.

From this brief statement I learned: 1) that I could speak to Sidi about anything. He doesn't shy away from any topic, including sex; 2) that making love is important in the Sufi path. It is how we water the tree of our relationship. This path isn't anything like celibate paths; and 3) that Sidi is grounded, practical and pragmatic.

Love relationships are sacred and holy. Sidi tells us that they are the culmination of the Sufi path. He writes in "Beloveds of God" in *Conversations in the Zawiya* (pp 24–28) "I have given you many subjects before to help you to know yourself and to find the key to open the hidden treasure inside you. After you have walked in the way and lifted the veils of darkness to see the light of God, He brings you a step higher to see Him in the face of your beloved. The understanding of God and all that His love means to you is completed by the sharing of the deep secret love with another. It is putting the essence of all the teachings, all the books, all the sciences, and all that God has given to you into manifestation through the love you share with your beloved. Everything before has been a preparation for seeing the light of God in the eye of your beloved."

The goal of the love relationship is unity with each other and with Allah, all at the same time. Sidi writes that the man in unity "does not make a difference between her and him, and she does not make a difference between him and her. They are one. There are no numbers in the truth. From the picture I have given you, and from the religion of your soul, the soul of God and of the guide, send mercy to your beloved because in this giving you are sending mercy for yourself." ("Beloveds of God")

He goes on to say, "Life in the marriage of beloveds is for each to be holy, and to care about one another. This marriage is like a holy tree whose roots grow deep into the earth, and the earth is the heart of God. How do you nourish this tree? By giving it love and clean water; water that has been cleansed of all the troubles of this world. It is necessary for the tree to grow strong in order to give shade to all the lovers of God who are beneath it. When nourished, her roots will grow deep into the earth, becoming all the qualities of God, covering the universe with His essence. This is the Tree of Life and it is necessary for it to be nourished with the love of God. Then it will give the holiest of fruits with His permission and have the sweetest flowers, because it comes from one source." ("Beloveds of God") What a lofty goal!

Abd al-Qadir Davies and I teach the peacemaking master's program at USHS. We have made this teaching on love and relationships our primary focus under Sidi's direction. We emphasize the importance of healing marriages, families and bringing the love to them. Sidi told us that there is no peace in the world, if there's no peace and love in the home and the family. Peace has to begin there.

There are many keys to forming successful, loving relationships including communication, deep listening, growing the love and walking through the stations of love, especially within marriage and parenthood. Another key aspect is **identity.** This is often the cause of strife within all kinds of relationships. We all have many identities. These are part of our nafs or ego. Within relationships, people naturally have different identities. This includes gender, values, roles, world views and socio-economic status. Identity itself is not the cause of our challenges. It is our **attachment** to our identities that makes us clash with each other.

For example, the woman and man fight because they are focused entirely on how different they are from each other in their gender. He is comfortable in his mind, and she is more at home in her emotions. They speak a different language stemming from this difference. As a result, they do not understand each other and they cannot get on the same page. Here the attachment to their gender, to "that's just the way I (or men) am," is the problem. If they could hold that identity loosely and make space around it inside, they could more readily get into their partner's "shoes" and see what things look like through their eyes. When we move into spaciousness and hold our identities loosely, we can more readily empathize with the other. Empathy creates connection, and connection creates love.

Allah sends me many couples and families in my private practice who are in need of help with their relationships. I have recently been working with a variety of couples who are in turmoil, and their love is in danger of being totally destroyed. In most cases they are mired in blame, accusations, misunderstandings, always being right, making the other wrong, trying to win and hopelessness. They are focused on what they see as vast differences between them and cannot find their common ground. They are stuck in their identities. This is the picture of relationships that come from the limited and limiting nafs or ego. It is mostly a struggle with very little love or harmony. This is very painful for the couples themselves, and it is also heart-wrenching for me to witness them in this state.

The level of strife and conflict I've encountered with these couples is reminiscent of my own marriage with Wadude many decades ago. We were also caught up in our identities, in being right and making the other wrong, constantly arguing, blaming and criticizing. Our drama took the form of my running down the street in the dead of night in my nightgown at my wits' end one time, or yelling at each other in the woods outside our cabin where no one was around to hear us another time. During those years, we were close to splitting up several times. It was agonizing, to say the least.

Since then, through our Sufi studies, we have learned many things that make our relationship work: the value of listening and communicating so that we really hear each other and get inside each other's world and heart; how to let go of the need to be right and to let love be the winner; how to get out of our nafs and bow our hearts in surrender to each other and how to make tawba or forgiveness and return to our connection with Allah.

I've also learned firsthand the importance of distinguishing between the world of the nafs/ego, where we want what we want regardless of the other person and their needs, and the world of the heart, where we want for the other what we want for ourselves. This is the beginning of true altruism and the beginning of love.

Getting to the place in our spiritual development where the world of the heart is natural and well-established inside of us, was a major turning point in our relationship. It was at this point that our need to be right and to win dissolved and the love took a front seat. That was our switch from the nafs to the heart. It was also at this point that we could understand and make real the notion that it is never about the other person.

These two working hypotheses that guide Wadude and me have made a huge difference for us:

1. **It's never about the other person.** Look in the mirror whenever you are in separation.

   As Sidi writes in *The Realty of Gnosis* (pp 24–26), everything that manifests to you is from you, for you and is you. So we've learned to look in the mirror when something happens that triggers us, and to focus on our own growth and purification rather than on trying to change the other person. In "Beloveds of God," he writes, "God says know that your wife is your mirror, and through her reflection you can see yourself. If she remains in your heart, you can see Me through the eye of your heart, but only if you care for this heart and send her love."

2. **You can either be right OR be in the love,** but you can't have both at the same time, because love and being right cannot coexist. Why?

Both of these principles come from our understanding of the nafs and the heart, and how those two realities affect relationships. Being right lives in the nafs or ego self, the part of us that is ruled by desire, preferences, and needs. It wants what it wants and only cares about others when they serve or help our own desires and purpose. Nafs is always essentially in separation. It cannot know love because nafs is only concerned about itself.

The heart, on the other hand, is the part of us that is capable of **connecting** with others and, therefore, can know love. As we journey on the path to God, our heart opens and deepens until we have iman or faith, and the sign of faith is that we want for another what we want for ourselves. This is the beginning of love and true connection with others. Through spiritual development over time, the nafs recedes, the heart and soul unfold and their reality takes over.

This journey is not just about outer behaviors. For love to be born, an inner shift to a different world is needed. Ultimately, the only way out of the turmoil of the nafs and the chaos and drama in this earthly world is Allah. Therefore, our personal connection and union with Allah are fundamental to building the love between us.

An example of the nafs wanting what it wants:

In a relationship, it is very common for people to want their partners to be how they want them to be, how they think they *should* be or how they *need* them to be. For example, most women want to be with a man whom they consider to be safe and trustworthy. This is usually a bottom line for women. A safe man, according to this picture, is soft, warm, in touch with his feelings and contains her completely. If at times, the man is also strong, virile and even controlling, the woman thinks that this is a deal-breaker because she doesn't feel safe with him when he's like that. She also often wants him to earn a certain amount of money to support her needs. This is a classic struggle over identity.

In my case, I wanted Wadude to be like both these pictures. I thought that he should be strong and virile, and soft and in touch with his emotions. In fact, for many years I wasn't even seeing him. I wasn't seeing who he is. I remember the exact day that my pictures of him cracked. We were hiking up a mountain and he was ahead of me. I looked up the trail at him from behind, and suddenly it was like a shape-shift happened: my pictures of what I wanted him to be, along with my disappointment when he wasn't living up to my pictures, just dissolved. It was like a veil was pulled away and I was shown who he is underneath his nafs and under the pictures that my nafs had of him. It was a huge revelation. I felt like I needed to pinch myself to get my bearings on reality. From that moment, his true self became more and more apparent to me, and with this awareness came tremendous appreciation of him. From that time, my pictures about him gradually faded away.

Recently, in a healing session with a similar woman, after I recited some holy prayers and verses, she said she felt "bathed in light and sees her husband as his own person. My happiness is not dependent on him. He's separate from me. I can love him as he is…I'm more at peace and have more faith inside. There's no fear, worry or pain. They're not gone, but I can see a bigger plan and I trust it."

I also remember another key turning point in our relationship: the time when we both stopped needing to be right. I guess that something changed in our nafs/ego self, so that we didn't need to win anymore and we could just surrender to whatever the other one said or did without trying to change or control it. This was very liberating and was the point when almost all of our struggles ended.

Once very early in our path with Sufism, when Sidi was staying at our house, he ordered us to say only "yes" to each other all the time for three weeks. It seemed like an impossible task, but we took up the challenge and followed his guidance. It was downright transformative and life-changing. Before then, I think we were mainly focused on our own thoughts and desires. We didn't really hear each other or consider the validity of what each other said or wanted. Once Sidi delivered the order to say only "yes" for three weeks, we had to catch ourselves over and over and interrupted our normal patterns. There were many times that our instincts were to disagree or say "no." However, we didn't let this happen. Little by little, something shifted between us. The need to prove ourselves faded and a new harmony blossomed between us. It was amazing to exist in that field of harmony together. This was very new for us. It took us some time to reach the point of trusting each other enough to say "yes" continuously.

Things are so different for us now, that it seems like light years ago on another planet. We're so grateful that we're far removed from that experience. We both think that this transformation is largely due to the teachings Sidi has given us, our walking on the Sufi path and his guidance and protection.

The icing on the cake was when we gained familiarity with and entered into the world of the soul. This enabled us to see each other as beautiful creations of God and precious jewels who deserve all the love from God and from each other. From that point, it is only a short journey to unity with each other. Only in God's world, is there union.

Sidi says, "My sons and daughters, if you knew what God has given to you, you would not do or say anything to break the heart of your beloveds. The key to living a life with a beloved is to give each other what each needs. I am sure that if everyone does all that I have said, he will live this day in the garden, and feel peace in any place and in any religion. This message knows no difference between people or religion. There is no life like this life, because you live all the time with God and pray all your time with God." ("Beloveds of God")

# Nura Laird, M.Ed.

Nura Laird earned her B.A. from Smith College and her M.Ed. from the University of Massachusetts. She has been married to John Wadude Laird for over 46 years, and they have two wonderful adult daughters, a son-in-law and a baby grandson.

Since 1977, Nura has been a student of spiritual healing and Sufism, the age-old Islamic mystical path of wisdom and love. Nura is a faculty member and chair of the Department of Peacemaking at The University of Spiritual Healing and Sufism.

Nura was involved in the alternative school movement between 1970 and 1995. She co-founded and taught at two alternative schools, and was director of one for 12 years. This school is now internationally recognized for innovation and excellence in pre- through middle school education. During those years, she created numerous innovative educational programs, published articles, was a featured speaker on radio and television, and a guest lecturer in several universities, promoting progressive values in education, parenting, and family healing. She spearheaded a formal research study in spiritually-based parenting and family healing which became the Ph.D. dissertation of one of her students.

She is also a professional mediator with extensive experience in community and family mediation as well as a number of counseling modalities. She and her co-professor, Dr. John Abd al-Qadir Davies, created a unique model of peacemaking that integrates conventional mediation with the teachings of Sufism and Sufi healing. This method facilitates healing and transformation on the mental, emotional and spiritual levels—peacemaking from the inside out.

Nura maintains a private practice in Northern California, working in person and remotely by phone or Skype, and also leads seminars internationally. Her personal, but not exclusive, focus is helping couples and families, friends and co-workers return to love and harmony. Working with individuals and groups, she provides a safe, gentle, holy space in which to learn, transform, and heal.

# *Finally Telling the Truth*

# Donna Jamila Crews, M.Div.

Thank God I was too far along for the abortion option. When my out-of-wedlock pregnancy was confirmed in 1967, I was rushed off to an unwed mothers' home. The memory is so vivid—like yesterday, instead of 50 years ago—holding my infant daughter, examining her toes and fingers and her little face, for the first and, I thought, for the last time. I was 18.

My emotions went underground. After her birth, I returned to my life in a small town, population 2,000, as though nothing had happened. Maid of honor at my best friend's wedding. Then right on to college. Subject dropped, like a hot potato.

Fast forward. In 1970, after my boyfriend came back from his military service, we were married. In 1975, when I was 27, my second daughter Amy was born. That was when the lying began. When someone asked me how many children I had, I replied, 'one.' In 1980 and 1982, my sons Casey and Lynn were born. The ache in my heart was alive, though it stayed dormant. Over the years, how many times was I asked how many children I had? I have no idea, but too many.

In 1999, at the end of my first year of Sufi University, the tide turned. Allah sent me an angel. I met a woman, Janie, who became my best friend. She worked in adoption, and she suggested that we go to the courthouse in Austin and search through the volumes and volumes of records for girls born in 1967, one of whom would be my daughter. A team of four went through the records, compiling a list of 25 names. I did some follow-up on them, but got nowhere, and finally let it rest.

In the spring of 2001, I believe that Allah decided to give me another nudge. A woman walked into a Unity Church where I worked. I happened to be sitting in the reception area and greeted her. This woman, named Paula, knew Janie and had learned from her that I had been looking for my daughter I had given up for adoption. She asked permission "to do a search," and of course, I agreed. I still don't know how she did it, but later that same afternoon she called me. She said that my daughter was Lara Lee Davis Hogg, living in San Diego at the naval base with her husband, who was in the Navy.

Paula suggested I call the naval base and ask to talk to a chaplain. I called and was connected to someone called Chaplain Mike. I told him that I was looking for my daughter, whom I had relinquished as an infant. I gave him Lara Lee's name. He abruptly said he would call me back, and hung up. He did not call back. Later that afternoon, I went over to my daughter Amy's house. Casey and Lynn were also there. I called Chaplain Mike again, and this time he said he knew Lara Lee. We were so excited! Amy asked Lara Lee's favorite flower. Casey asked if she could palm a basketball. Lynn asked what her favorite car was!

Chaplain Mike suggested that we write Lara Lee a letter, send it to him, and he would give it to her. So, we did. We sent letters and pictures. Word spread through the family that we had found our long-lost daughter/sister.

In mid-July of 2001, Lara Lee's husband Wes called Amy, suggesting that we fly out to San Diego for a surprise meeting with Lara Lee on her 33rd birthday. On July 24, 2001, Amy and I were waiting a little distance from the entrance of the Coronado Inn, watching for my older daughter to arrive. What a suspenseful moment!! We saw a tall, dark-haired woman walk into the restaurant.

A bit later, a waitress came out to get us and showed us to a table, where Wes was just telling Lara Lee that her mother and sister were standing right behind her! She stood up, turned around, and not missing a beat, hugged both of us! When I asked her to take off her sunglasses, I saw green eyes just like mine! Lara Lee and I are the only ones in the family with green eyes.

Two weeks after Amy and I met with Lara Lee on her 33rd birthday, Lara Lee flew to Texas to meet her brothers Casey and Lynn, her biological Dad, and her grandmother, Memer. A few weeks later, Amy flew to see Lara Lee. Amy and Lara Lee dressed up and went to a Navy ball, where people asked if they were twins!!

Well, you say, "What did Sufi U have to do with this reunion?" I credit Sufi U with cleaning my heart and soul of the guilt of giving up a baby for adoption. Then Lara Lee came to me. Allah did need to send a few angels my way — Allah was very patient. Looking back, Sufi U provided the safety and then the healing for my heart to let go of the pain, and open to receive Lara Lee into my life.

Now, 16 years after reconnecting with Lara Lee, I love being in the presence of all four of my kids, and watching them be together. My heart rests easy. My soul is at peace. I love for people to ask how many children I have, cherishing my reply — "FOUR"

But back to Chaplain Mike. Chaplain Mike was the pastor where Lara Lee attended church, and he knew she was adopted. When I called him that morning out of the blue, Chaplain Mike immediately called Lara Lee. And when I called him back that afternoon from Amy's house, Lara Lee was in Chaplain Mike's office. She heard our excitement and our questions about her. Lara Lee decided, right then and there, that she wanted to meet all of us!

How can you patiently wait for your silver lining? First, look for ways to heal the pain. Then, be patient. Keep the faith. Allah's will be done.

I am blessed.

## Donna Jamila Crews, M.Div.

Hi, I'm Donna Jamila Crews... Early in my career, prior to USHS, I worked as an executive director and counselor in healing programs for adults and youth experiencing alcohol and drug abuse and addiction.

My career with USHS began in 1998. Completing the basic 3-year USHS program in 2001, I spent many years helping people heal, using the Sufi principles and skills that I learned at Sufi U. I continued as a Teaching Assistant and worked on various Masters degrees offered by USHS.

After retiring, I passionately pursued—and achieved—a Masters of Divinity at USHS, specializing in Peacemaking. I moved through my avoidance of conflict by learning mediation skills. I now feel more equipped to help create world peace in our current political climate.

I live in Seattle, with my daughter, Amy, and nine-year-old grandson, Cannon. I moved here in 2012 from Austin, where I lived for 23 years. I was blessed to help start the Sufi community in Austin in 1998. I helped the community to grow and mature, until I moved to Seattle in 2012.

I have a Business—BoomerWomanBucketList.com.

I help Boomer women make these years their best years.

A new website, CreatingInterfaith.com, is now live. Creating Interfaith helps people of different faiths connect hearts, creating peace, rather than focusing on differences and creating conflict. I look forward to helping our global community connect hearts, by creating peace in these turbulent times.

# *Speaking the Truth with Love*

# Robert Ibrahim Jaffe, M.D., M.D.(H), D.D.

This is one of my favorite stories of my relationship with Sidi. In Sufism, the jalal teachings, or the difficult teachings, are often considered to be higher than the jamal, or the easier teachings; the beautiful teachings. Although I did not always like the jalal teachings, they were significant for me. They changed so much in my own consciousness that I think it's worth talking about. It demonstrates the nature of Sufism in a very core place.

I am like everyone in that I like truth. I like to stand for truth and speak about truth. I think that truth is one of the key things of life.

One time I was lecturing to a group of people at a regional Sufi school. I wanted to tell a story about education. I was trying to talk to the audience about what that education looked like. At the time, my own child was in Waldorf School. We were working through issues of Waldorf for her. This was because there were some places where she wasn't integrating well into the system.

When I looked at what was going on, I found that she was doing some of the patterning work. However, she didn't want to do some of the things that they were teaching her. I asked her why. She felt that as she was learning the patterning, there was somehow a control coming in that was affecting her mind in a way that she didn't like. However, she didn't want to accept that. Since we had spent a great deal of time in Sufism learning about subtle light and the subtle world behind things, she was able to articulate that.

I said, "Does it come from the exercise, or where does it come from?"

She said, "No, I don't think it's the exercise itself." She said she thought it came more from something going on behind, that was affecting her consciousness. It might have been coming from one of the teachers at the school itself. But she said, "I'm not comfortable with it. I don't want to do it." I support that position because I believe that children are very wise and have understanding that exceeds what most of us really recognize.

Therefore, I wanted to talk to this group about the educational system that we have. The intent was to convey the understanding that ultimately what we really want is Divine education. It means that much of what we learn, has to do with things that may, in some ways, program our minds in a way that isn't right. In this case, I felt that my daughter was telling me there was a programming coming in which was controlling her mind. It was supposed to be in a way that would make her free, but, in fact, was another form of control.

As I studied educational systems, I learned that the American education system was introduced about 1918, at the time of WW1. It was based on an indoctrination process that was put into place to help people to go into the military. This indoctrination system was listen, learn, obey, do what you're told and don't fight back. Part of this system is still operating today in the traditional school systems. This is something that I don't think any teacher would be aware of. I certainly think that teachers in the system itself are unaware of it. Most of them would be appalled, if they ever thought that was what was going on.

However, that was the way the system had been created and is still being practiced today. In many classes, the message to students is, "Do what you're told and learn what you're taught." There is little room for real discussion.

I was talking about this in the class. I didn't realize it, but I had many teachers in the class. I spoke about the educational process, control in Waldorf and how the education system was being used to indoctrinate people. I really created a lot of pain in teachers who were there. These were teachers who were trying desperately to free their students and to teach them good things. I was telling them that their system was actually indoctrinating people. They were very hurt and angry. I said, "Well, I'm telling you the truth. I'm telling you this is how it was created. It's still operating this way, and this is why they did it."

Instead of bringing liberation to, these teachers, it brought a lot of rage for them. They felt judged. They felt put in a box. They said, "We're not doing that!" There was this anger that I brought up in this situation, which actually was not my intention.

Later on when Sidi came back, his statement to me was, "I don't stand with Ibrahim and what Ibrahim said, and I'm angry about what he said." It was very embarrassing. However, my statement was, "I'm standing for the truth. I've told you the truth. Why would you be upset about an expression of truth?"

Later that night, I went to see Sidi. He didn't want to talk to me for a while. However, he finally came out and I said, "What is the reason that you're angry with me for speaking about truth?" He said to me, "Ibrahim, the truth is fine. There's no trouble with the truth. What I had trouble with, is the insensitivity on your part. It was because you didn't realize that what you were saying hurt the hearts of people who were trying their best." He said, "Shouldn't you be wise enough to be able to bring forth truth in a way that honors and respects where people are and doesn't create a situation of creating pain for them? Shouldn't it create a situation of uplifting them and taking them into a place where they can honor the truth themselves without feeling made wrong, in reaction or judged?"

I realized that there was a higher level than just speaking truth. It involved the understanding of the impacts of the truth on people. What was being asked with Sufism was to have the deepest respect and honor for where people were, their position, how they think and what they believe. We need to honor that truth like a tree that needs to grow. But if you put something into someone, that they're not ready for or they don't agree with, all that you do is create pain and separation for them. I had missed that in my desire to speak the truth. This was a very critical moment for me in my own walking. I realized that everything I spoke about needed to honor and respect people. I needed to respect their process, where they came from and value where they were at. Sufism was about understanding truth and purifying our places of untruth. It had to be done through a system of deepest respect and valuing other people. I've come to understand how God holds all creation with the deepest love, respect and honor. It is done with the deepest patience, support and love with the willingness to view every situation full of mercy and every situation full of compassion. It is also important to give everything its due and everything its time as it matures and unfolds.

This became one of the highest teachings that I received. It is still something that I think about every day. I always try, as a Sufi teacher, to really examine whether I'm honoring the people I'm with and valuing their process. I want to ensure that whatever it is that I may want to teach or whatever Sufism brings to the world is done with the greatest respect, and mobility. It must also value all traditions and honor them in a way that God would honor them.

**Robert Ibrahim Jaffe, M.D., M.D.(H), D.D.**

Robert Ibrahim Jaffe, M.D., M.D.(H), D.D., is the past President of The University of Spiritual Healing & Sufism and a faculty member. Dr. Jaffe is a licensed medical doctor who, for the last 25 years, has pioneered advanced energetic and spiritual healing in the United States. Dr. Jaffe received his medical degree from the University of Illinois and practiced allopathic, complimentary and homeopathic medicine in Arizona and Hawaii. He now resides in northern California.

After studying many different spiritual paths, Dr. Jaffe found Sufism to be a true path of the heart. It is through the beautiful techniques of Sufi Spiritual Healing that he has seen the deepest and most complete healings occur on the physical, energetic and spiritual levels. This spiritual healing works together with traditional and non-traditional medical care.

Dr. Jaffe founded the Jaffe Institute (now known as The University of Spiritual Healing and Sufism) in June, 2000, to bring his comprehensive synthesis of medical, energetic, and spiritual healing to professionals and lay people who want to heal in a complete and holy way by deepening their understanding of why people become sick and what can be done to resolve their illness.

Dr. Jaffe is a master healer, spiritual teacher and Sufi Murshid of the Shadhiliyya Sufi Order, who has completed over 40,000 healings and helped thousands of people to walk further in their personal journeys.

Dr. Jaffe brings an ocean of love, wisdom and healing to those people who are seeking to find the truth and reality of their beings.

# *Humility:*
# *An Essential Thread in the Carpet of Life*
# **Paul Hamid Werder**

My two business partners left our company one day. This occurred in the mid-nineties and they said they just wanted to pursue their aspirations for service and success on their own. One of them reminded me, "Paul you don't respect me," on her way out the door. I had been reassuring her for two years that I did respect her, but it was to no avail. This was a difficult pill to swallow, because I had been earning my living as a teambuilding and leadership consultant for over 15 years. I, therefore, decided to seek outside help and attended a four-day workshop called Working Relationships. It was a small group, the facilitator was quite good, and the material felt empowering. What floored me, however, was the morning of the fourth day, another participant approached me and said, "Paul, I don't think you really respect me."

I had hardly spoken to her all week! I could not imagine how she had come to the same conclusion in three days that my former partner hadn't been able to convey to me for over two years. The facilitator suggested that I find an energy healer to help me clear away my "unresolved stuff" that was inadvertently damaging my relationships.

My healer was a student in what is now the University of Spiritual Healing and Sufism. She helped me open my heart by repeating the words "my heart" over and over again. She patiently kept encouraging me to go deeper when I had no idea what she meant. I surprised both of us when I had a very cathartic experience of coughing, crying, and finally laughing uncontrollably about some bad memories from the past and worries about the future.

I told my wife, Jenell, about my experience and she called the healer for her own appointment. At her first session, the healer took one look at Jenell and said, "You are a healer; you should attend the school where I am studying." Jenell was taken aback, but was soon flying to California for weeks at a time to study Sufi healing.

I kept up with my own regular healing sessions, but for a year or so I simply saw it as a means to an end. I just wanted to be more successful with my business consulting. Then Jenell invited me to attend three days of her school session focused on Divine Marriage. During the final hour of our drive down to the school, I had severe chest pains that I had never felt before. I wondered aloud if I was having a heart attack and suggested we visit a hospital. Jenell knew better, and I later realized I was simply freaking out physically because I was not very skilled at dealing with my emotions. On some inner level, I must have known that everything was about to change.

On the first morning of the Divine Marriage session, Ibrahim Jaffe walked into the room with more than a hundred students and guests. He spoke to a student privately for a moment, then turned his attention onto the group before looking directly at me sitting in the second row. He smiled, and asked, "What is your question?" I hadn't put my hand up, but there I was fumbling for words with the microphone someone had just put into my hands. I explained that I was here with my wife to learn about divine marriage.

Ibrahim gave me a lengthy and puzzling metaphorical response. He described me as a planet revolving around a sun and that I needed to become a sun in my own right. I was puzzled because I had my own business and place in the world, but I eventually understood he wasn't talking about that. Spiritually, I had left the tradition I was raised with, and until meeting Jenell, was no longer interested in the topic. I had lately been relying on her to reintroduce me to different versions of spirituality that I had found uplifting. He was right. It was time for me to get myself into the game that really mattered.

Those three days were eye opening enough for me that I signed up for the Year 1 class beginning a few months later. Before that began, however, Jenell and I decided to take a long weekend to drive down and visit one of the Sufi guide's classes. When we arrived, we discovered the guide, Sidi, wasn't teaching the only day we could be there. We were told, however, that we could visit with him at his son's home another 45 minutes away.

I had been hoping to anonymously check this all out a bit further sitting in the back of the room. However, I again found myself sitting directly in front of a holy man, this time from Jerusalem, asking me what questions I had. I was speechless and we just sat there in silence for a minute until he said, "Say after me, I promise Allah...." Jenell had forewarned me that he'd ask me to take the Sufi promise and it was clear that my heart was ready, at least to him. He gave me the name Hamid. When I asked what it meant he said, "The one who asks for the love of God and receives the love of God." That sounded great to me, but my anxiety was acting up on the drive home again. The prayer beads he gave me broke and I had to gather up 100 beads from the floor of the car. I wondered if these beads were defective, but Jenell reminded me that I tended to do things, even praying, more intensely than necessary.

About a year later, I was in class with Ibrahim teaching again. He was giving a very interesting lecture on arrogance that day, and I thought of a few people I wished could hear this teaching. When he finished the talk, however, he said, "Hamid, come on up to the front of the class." I noticed the microphone shaking in my hand as I looked at the class when, once again, I hadn't asked a question. This time, as the poster child for arrogance, I was thinking to myself. He compassionately worked me through my shakiness, as he asked me a very challenging question, "Hamid, who would you be if you let go of your sense of inadequacy?"

I mumbled a few answers and he engaged a couple of students to assess which ones might be my real answer. Ibrahim finally said I hadn't gotten to the deepest truth yet and asked me to go deeper. As I stood there, with that "go deeper" comment again, the voice of my heart came through this time. I realized how empowering these teachings really were, and also how skilled the teachers were. Finally, I responded with a soft voice, "If I could do anything, without any restrictions, I would love to be a spiritual teacher and represent what Sidi is bringing to all of us." Ibrahim smiled and replied, "I think that's right for you."

That conversation was very powerful. It illuminated the two sides of a coin I had struggled with my whole life. In one scenario, I doubted I was good enough, and in the next moment I felt superior to those I was working with. My former partner had been right. I had been more judgmental than respectful with her. Reading and writing Sidi's books had taught me that these teachings can wash all of that "stuff" out of our hearts until we are the embodiment of love and the other beautiful qualities. To be free of my self-consciousness and self-importance was both inspiring and exciting to contemplate! The next few years felt like I'd been let out of a self-imposed prison.

My journey continued very nicely as we grew a community in Portland, Oregon. I was invited to play a beginner's role on the faculty. However, I occasionally needed a bit of help from my guide. It almost always came in an indirect or even mystical manner. I was never one to sit privately with Sidi and ask him a straightforward question.

For example, one of Sidi's practices at our school sessions was to publicly announce teacher ranks and give those promises in return for a sacrifice or donation. I had a great deal of admiration for the faculty members and started to subtly strive to be in the same rank as my mentors. After all, the Portland community was doing quite well at the time, a little voice inside whispered to me. One session Sidi read off the names of the first group to be given the promise in their new rank. My name was included in that senior group where I was aspiring to find myself. I was quietly overjoyed, but then some unexpected business came up that consumed Sidi's attention for nearly 45 minutes. Finally, with my hopeful self all set, he read the list again without my name mentioned. Instead, I was called up in the next group and my nasty internal voices were ablaze, as I took that promise with a dozen or more others.

A few minutes later, I saw what was happening. Sidi had seen me striving for public recognition and he had gotten me, and gotten me good. I felt ashamed and very remorseful. That evening I knew I would not be able to sleep, so I sat up in the hotel room for almost three hours doing the Tawba prayer for returning to our connection to God. Finally, my prayers released my shame and mental self-abuse. I eventually even laughed at myself and felt gratitude for his clever way of teaching me another powerful lesson. And sure enough, the following day, Sidi found a way to let me know he had seen that I had done my Tawba and cleaned another layer of arrogance—without saying one word directly to me.

Along the way, Sidi put out a qualities book and I learned that Hamid was one of the ninety-nine qualities. It literally meant the Praiseworthy. It occurred to me that the interpretation Sidi had given to my name originally, was precisely what I needed at the time—to ask for and receive the love of God. But the deeper significance of this name to me didn't come along for several years after I learned this literal translation.

I was at a school session talking with a close friend when I suddenly looked up on a video screen that highlighted the word Alhumduli'llah. Alhumduli'llah is a word we use to acknowledge God as the Source of everything that is going well in our lives. It was like halleluiah to me and I had never really thought about this word's actual translation. But when I read the English words beneath it for this first time, I said to my friend, "Wow, what a beautiful principle that is!" She looked at me funny and said, "Well, duh, that's the root of your name Hamid, no wonder it's so beautiful for you."

I read the words again: All Praise is Only for Allah. I got choked up at the words All and Only. This was my core lifelong lesson. My walking in this world was to get my "self" out of the way to be an expression of love. I remembered the first question and answer in my Catechism from 1st grade at the Catholic school I attended. Why did God make us? God made us to know, love, and serve Him. My Sufi path had brought me full circle to the same teaching I had memorized as a child, but now I was learning it in a much deeper, experiential way.

Later that evening, I was reflecting more on the spiritual upbringing I had left behind. I remembered the pictures of the saints with a glow around their heads. I had thought this glow was just an artist's metaphorical rendition that these people were holy. I now realized that this glow was the same light we all experience at times during a healing session or when praying. My Sufism was now, at the deepest level, the same path as my original Christianity. All the prophets really did carry the same message! Most importantly, this Divine Light is available to every person who finds the door of surrendering their "ego-stuff" to Allah. We all are amazingly beautiful at our soul level! This is what I was meant to learn from the name Hamid.

These discoveries, unfortunately, do not mean we have arrived. We remember and we forget. It is an infinite learning curve. We are forever invited to return to Alhumduli'llah.

Years later, our country struggled through an economic recession. My income was down 35% and I needed a home equity loan to make it through the year. I was worrying about this on my flight to teach at the school, when I remembered that Sidi would be there. I thought if I was ever going to ask him a direct question for help, this was my time. To make sure I could get my question across completely, I decided to ask his translator to help.

As I walked around the corner of the building when I first arrived, Sidi saw me and said, "Ahhh Hamid, when he trusts Allah the whole world will open to him." I said, "Thank you Sidi, but I have a question for you." He nodded and I went off to find the translator. I even asked the translator to tell Sidi to please let me take a minute to finish my question before responding. After listening for a minute or two about my financial struggles, Sidi gave a detailed analysis of how President Obama was going to close the military sites around the world in the next three months, and I would be seeing my business pick up by then.

As I watched the news for three months, none of what Sidi told me happened. I realized he'd gotten me again. Even though he had no reason to know I was coming to the school that day, or had a question, he'd given me my answer before I said hello. I needed to deepen my trust in Allah. He must have been quite amused that I missed the answer, because I was overly focused on making sure he would hear my question. Humbled again, I went to work on my trust until I was seeing my world open up again.

Unfortunately, I had my own pictures of what it meant to have the world open for me. A few years later, I was invited to be on a team of Distinguished Fellows at Case Western Reserve University to write a book about spirituality and business. I was very excited and hopeful that this would be an opportunity to bring our teachings to a wider audience and to personally become more economically secure. The book, *Flourishing Enterprise,* turned out well and even had a beautiful description of the Remembrance in it.

But my pictures were not at all what this project was about for me. I did not navigate the team dynamics well. My ego got knocked around by a couple of my teammates, and regrettably I'd given them a bit of ammunition to do so. I tried my best to hold my alignment, but my health became significantly compromised when I couldn't trust Allah through these challenges. Once again, I was humbled. I needed to learn to have gratitude for the times of hardship we are given when we have more ego-tendencies to clean.

I did not recover my health quickly or easily, but the blessings were just as significant as the hardship. One sleepless night when I was very fearful that my affliction would be with me indefinitely, I prayed and prayed asking for help. The answer in my heart was loud and clear, "You have everything you need." I cannot describe how much relief that message gave me. I doubled down on my commitment to trust Allah. I took the example of two friends born into Sufism and devoted myself to a much more conscious prayer practice. I deeply embraced these lines from Fawzia's book, *Divine Names,* in the chapter on "Hamid": "To admit one's own ignorance in the face of the Divine is a great and difficult step. It is a step of dissolution. It is the deep knowledge that all things, all beings are connected with one another. Then you stop being the center and become an essential thread in the carpet of life instead."[1]

During this time of hardship in my life, Sidi passed away. I was grateful for his life of service. I was happy it was his time to be with Allah. I felt no loss because his teaching has always been to "thank Allah" and not rely on Sidi, the humble man who brought us His message. Reflecting upon this core teaching, I believe Sidi was in a station where he could help Allah walk us. But it is Allah Who walks us. It occurs every day with the events of our lives when we are awake enough to notice God's signs in every experience we are given. This is how we know, love and serve God. Sidi got us started in a way that was unimaginable to me when I first said, "I promise Allah…" Now we have the teachings and one another. We have an extraordinary opportunity to find the peace, love, and wisdom already within our hearts.

After almost twenty years on this path, I am simply left with gratitude that Allah has provided me with my beloved Jenell, our Sufi teachings and so many beautiful fellow travelers. I aspire to find my spirituality coming to life every day for the rest of my life. I find much joy supporting others to bring these teachings into the world in their own unique way. I am devoted to learning All Praise is Only for Allah. It is the life we are meant to live. Alhumduli'llah.

---

1        *Divine Names: The 99 Healing Names of the One Love,* by Rosina-Fawzia Al-Rawi

**Paul Hamid Werder**

Paul Hamid Werder has been a successful consultant in organizational change and leadership development for over 30 years. He is president of LionHeart Consulting, Inc., and a faculty member at the University of Spiritual Healing & Sufism in the Department of Spiritual Ministry.

Hamid has merged his traditional business acumen with spiritual healing skills to empower leaders to work from their hearts, as opposed to their egos. He supports his students to discover their unique God-given talents and express them completely with deep humility. His work with students at USHS focuses on developing the strength to walk in the world as a Sufi or spiritual healer. He helps students deepen their reliance on God, know their unique purpose and contribute to society in their own unique way.

Hamid is the author of two books, *Building Unity: Experiencing Love, Peace and Wisdom in Business and Daily Life,* and *Mastering Effectiveness.*

He also co-authored *Flourishing Enterprise: The New Spirit of Business* with eight other Distinguished Fellows from the Fowler Center for Business as an Agent of World Benefit at Case Western Reserve University.

# *Living in Unity When We Disagree*

# John Wadude Laird, MD

Within a couple of short years after Sidi came to the United States and was teaching our particular group of students, there was a Sufi school in Austin. I would guess that it was probably the first one. Sidi had called a group of about seven or eight people together. I was invited to attend, and it was very clear that he intended this group to take on leadership positions in our region and nationally without saying as much. He looked at all of us and he said, "I want there to be only unity in this group, no separation." For me it was very clear. It was like orders from the boss and our spiritual guide.

There were challenges in some of the relationships within the group. They were not challenges that I was experiencing directly, but ones that were obvious. I sat with this in my heart for many weeks, asking "How do we really live in unity with each other without making any separation?"

Fast forward to several weeks later: Sidi was staying at our house in Pope Valley, California. He was outside sitting smoking hookah as he usually did early in the morning. It was a time of prayer for him. I was in some other part of the house, thinking about this question in my heart. I was turning it over and over in my heart, and then I thought to myself, "I wonder if Sidi would be available in this moment to talk to me." It sounded like there were other people outside with him. I just wondered metaphorically, if the door was open to talk to him.

Then I got a very clear intuition that it was, but I immediately thought about it and said, "I'm not going to go out there." About 15 seconds later, somebody came into the room where I was and said, "Sidi would like to see you, Wadude." It was very clear to me that he had picked up what was going on. I, therefore, went out there, and sat down with this question in my heart. I noticed that one of the people sitting next to him, was actually someone who was not originally in this group of seven. However, it was someone who I was led to believe was part of the separation and who was expressing very strong opinions about someone else in the group. I thought to myself, "Oh gosh, I don't want to bring up this question out loud, because that could just create more separation."

So I went inside with my spirit, and I said, "Sidi teach me how you are in unity with people, even with people who are criticizing you openly." It was my understanding that one person in this group was criticizing Sidi openly. My eyes were closed, and I was sitting about three feet in front of him. Then, as soon as I put that thought out, and as soon as I asked that question, all of a sudden my heart was completely luminous. It was as if I was thousands of feet above the ocean surface, and on the surface way, way, way below was one of these people who was criticizing Sidi. It was as if the person was throwing a tantrum, thrusting, yelling and criticizing. Two things were immediately transmitted to me. One was that Sidi placed me in his heart. I saw that the criticism from this person had absolutely no impact on the vastness and the peace of his heart. It didn't ruffle anything inside of him.

Secondly, even deeper, the statement of his heart toward this person throwing tantrums in the ocean surface, was "This is my beloved student who I love completely and who I'm bringing to Allah." He was very full of love, and I was deeply touched. But about three seconds later, my own ego's reaction to this was, "No way does this person deserve that kind of loving treatment given what the person has been making in the world, making separation and accusations." I saw that this was my own darkness.

By that time in my relationship with my guide, I no longer wanted to be right. My heart's desire was more about, "Please show me." This was all done silently. I wasn't defending my darkness on the inner plane. My spirit was saying, "Please Sidi, show me how to really be in the peace. Show me how I can be in the peace." As soon as I said that, the light of healing went deep into my belly. Suddenly, this darkness came up and out of my lower belly and was released. I spontaneously leaned forward in my chair. I don't even remember what the particular issue was. Two seconds later, a little bit higher, another piece of darkness and judgment and arrogance, was coming up. It just released spontaneously from me. I bent even further from my chair, which was actually towards Sidi, because he had his hookah between us. He was really making the prayers with his hookah.

Another piece of constriction in my heart came up and out. As it came out, my heart expanded, and I bent so far forward, it was almost like I was moving into prostration to Allah. I almost fell out of my chair into his hookah. But I got the teaching immediately. The place of peace was to clear the places in my soul that were jealous and arrogant. It was also to allow compassion with real love. This whole process that I just described probably took 10 seconds from start to finish. In the spirit, I just thanked Sidi and got up and walked away. Not a word was exchanged between us.

As if to confirm the doubts of what I had experienced, Allah set up a very surprising conversation thirty seconds later. I was wandering around in the front of the house, just being with the healing that had happened. Ibrahim Jaffe had just driven up and parked his car in front of our house. He had no idea what had just happened. He walked up to me and said, "Wadude, your heart!" I said, "What about my heart?" He said, "I don't know what happened, but your heart is really carrying the unity right now." It was one of those gifts from Allah just to confirm that the experience I had been given. It was really a beautiful template for what we can do individually to clean the places in our being that cause separation. For me, it was envy, arrogance, judgment and things of that territory.

There is a specific Sufi teaching that relates to this story. The secret of the love of Allah is that each of us was created in perfection as an action of Allah's love. Allah's love and all of the Divine qualities reside deep in our hearts, in the secret of our hearts—the deepest love of our hearts. That is what we call the inheritance. It's the Divine treasure that we've inherited from Allah. The Sufi path is a beautiful teaching and a beautiful way of living in which Allah wants us to discover truth and to live in a world where your own heart is a garden. It is where you release all of the false identities and stories, false beliefs and self-limiting beliefs. It's where you begin to discover who you are in truth. You also begin to find your existence in the qualities of Allah. You become aware that everything you need is flowing to you from Allah moment by moment by moment.

These qualities flow through you, through the secret of your heart to all the dimensions of your being out into the world. You then begin your servitude to Allah and to be someone who really distributes pure Divine light in your own unique way.

I have always treasured that teaching from Sidi. It had a very, very profound impact in my life. I hope to be able to follow that teaching, wherever possible.

# John Wadude Laird, M.D.

Dr. John Wadude Laird, M.D., is a co-founder, past president and current faculty member of The University of Spiritual Healing & Sufism.

Dr. Laird has been on the forefront of the holistic medicine movement for forty years. Early in the movement, Dr. Laird noted that "body-mind-spirit" medicine generally lacked deeper understanding of spiritual transformation. In the early 1980's, he organized several major conferences exploring scientific and spiritual perspectives on healing, attended by over 5,000 people.

Dr. Laird founded the Great Smokies Medical Center and co-founded the Great Smokies Diagnostic Lab to expand innovative and comprehensive patient care options. Both organizations have been leaders in setting new standards in the practice of integrative medicine.

Dr. Laird's personal spiritual practice since 1977 has focused on Sufism which is based on deep and subtle understandings of the human heart and its relationship with God. As a co-founder, director and faculty member of The University of Spiritual Healing & Sufism, he played a leading role in shaping academic and clinical instruction on the application of the classical Sufi perspectives to facilitate spiritual healing.

He has provided personal healing sessions to thousands of people with a wide variety of physical, emotional and spiritual concerns. He has taught these approaches to several thousand people in the past twenty years, and is widely recognized as a sincere, engaging, fun and uniquely effective teacher.

# Illness as a Path to Spiritual Completion

# Rahima Susan Schmall, Ph.D., R.N.

*"If God said,*
*"Rumi, pay homage to everything*
*That has helped you*
*Enter my*
*Arms,"*
*There would not be one experience of my life,*
*Not one thought, not one feeling*
*Not any act, I*
*Would not*
*Bow*
*To"*

Author: Rumi
Book: *Love Poems from God*
Translator: Daniel Ladinsky

"To turn our will and our life over to the care of God as we understand Him" As I first listened to these words, they propelled me to ask myself, how can I surrender completely in this way? I was 20 years old in the early 1970s when I was introduced to the Twelve Steps of Al-Anon. At the same time, I discovered the prayer of St. Francis, which starts, "Make me an instrument of Your peace." These two phrases became the compass point for my life. I began to feel God's guidance bringing me home.

Later in the 1970's, I was introduced to Tibetan Buddhism. During the following twenty years, in which I immersed myself in the practice of meditation, the question of God and the desire to surrender to God, continued to haunt me. I found myself saying a prayer. "God, I will do anything to be one with You."

In 1987, as I was starting to write my doctoral dissertation in psychology, I became very ill with Chronic Fatigue Immune Dysfunction Syndrome and Environmental Illness. Six months later, I found myself bedridden, having to surrender my livelihood, school, and all the identities I believed defined my worth. As I let go, I discovered that my worth was not in what I did, but in who I am as a human being. This phase of my life lasted more than three years. I had to accept the possibility that the way I would serve the world was not as a meditation teacher and psychologist, but by allowing others to take care of me.

Even though I knew that the illness was an answer to my prayer, it took many years of bouncing between anger at myself to anger at God and blaming myself to blaming God, to see good in the hardship. Ultimately, I learned that God brings us exactly what we need to complete our journey home to Him.

Spiritual maturity involves seeing the deeper wisdom and finding peace in the midst of all life events. Physical illness, probably more than any other life event, strips away our attachments. It compels us to find our true inner nature rather than relying on beliefs for our identity. To become one with God and to surrender completely, we have to let go of everything that is "other" and our attachments to the created world, rather than the Creator. The Sufis call this "being in the world but not of it," and, in Sufism, the Path is what takes us there.

In 1991, I graduated from my Ph.D. program. I followed an inspiration from dreams and traveled to the Southwest, where I found a home in Santa Fe. I never thought I would be well enough to work again, but I began teaching at a local graduate school. Many days I was so tired, I would crawl out of bed, drive to work, go into the classroom and teach. Somehow, the teaching came from a place deep inside my being that was beyond the exhaustion and pain I lived with on a daily basis. After class, I would go home and crawl back into bed.

I slowly gained strength, but I never felt well. I bought a house, had a wonderful Shitzu, friends and work. On many levels, my life was far better than I had imagined possible with chronic illness. But what was the point? My heart still longed for complete surrender to God. I still trusted that these hardships were part of that surrender. Another prayer was, "Please bring me what I need to be with You."

I was then introduced to a Sufi healer. This man was different from the spiritual and energetic healers I had seen in the past. He embodied what I was searching for. He suggested I go to Los Angeles for a weekend workshop that would introduce me to Sufism and Sufi healing work. He also suggested I attend The University of Spiritual Healing and Sufism (then the Jaffe Institute), which was also located in California. These were big commitments. My mind kept saying, "No, too far to travel, too much money, I am content where I am." But out of my mouth came a "yes," because my heart knew I had found what I had been seeking. Six months later, this healer and his wife moved to be by the Sufi Retreat Center in Pope Valley, and a year later I followed.

I did not leave without struggle and fear. Here I was with Environmental Illness, living in a safe home and earning a living. Was I crazy to give it all up to move back to California, where the pollution had made me ill?

People often believe that a spiritual path should be easy and that the way should be laid out before us. The common belief is that if we are not given what we want, then either we did something wrong or there is something wrong with the path. We get discouraged in the face of obstacles and strong emotions that do not seem spiritual. Surrendering completely, however, means giving up our fears, our beliefs about ourselves and the world, pride and ego desires. It does not come without struggle. We hold these things, believing that they are who we are or what will make us safe. In Sufism, that struggle is called an inner "jihad" or war between our deep heart that wants God and our ego that wants control.

During my move back to California, there were days when I was terrified of letting go of the security that I had built for myself. Each day, I brought this fear into prayer and received healing work until I knew that my security was in God, not in what I had built for my life in Santa Fe. I began to experience waves of calm, relieving the terror and increasing my trust. I learned that true surrender is not about having everything go the way I want, but finding peace with all the challenges that present themselves.

We often create pictures of what will happen when we surrender. "If I give up my desire for money, I will be poor." "If I give up my need to be healthy, I will remain sick." Our minds go to polarities, but when we go into the heart and surrender, the path opens up in unexpected ways. The heart knows unity and can solve the unsolvable in unimaginable ways. Each time we embrace our inner struggle and choose the side of surrender, we come closer to God and the movement toward Him gets easier. One way to do this is through the practice of Remembrance. In this practice, we are reciting a Name of God or a phrase that helps us choose the side of surrender over beliefs.

One such Remembrance practice is the phrase, "La Illaha Il Allah," "There is no god but God." Our misbeliefs that we hold onto are the "god" or idol that needs to be surrendered. With the second part of the phrase, we are acknowledging that there is only one God or true reality. Finding where inside of our hearts that we hold the false belief, saying "la illaha il Allah" over and over again into that place in our heart, frees us from the constraints of beliefs into the vast reality of possibility that is God.

There is a Sufi saying, "He loved us first and then we loved Him." As human beings, we are born pure and we are created to know God. This is called "fitrah", which is our natural, inborn disposition toward good. The human being is unique in all of creation. We were created to know God and the desire to manifest the Divine qualities is innate. Healing is about opening back up to the purity in our hearts by letting go of all our veils of misconception.

We are born with this purity but as we are in the world and have experiences, we cover over this pure heart with interpretations and misunderstandings about ourselves, the world and God. We forget that the light of God shines in our hearts and that we were created to live in this light. Veils of misconception form easily. They may form from an event as simple as being in the crib while our mother, who is busy with another child, does not get to us as fast as we need. It may be as complex as sexual abuse or trauma. Either way, we create stories about the experience and then live those stories out. "I am not good enough." "Nobody is there for me." "The world is a dangerous place." The stories go on and on. We then selectively view future life experiences through that lens, keeping the ones that fit our story and ignoring the ones that might show us a different reality.

These stories lodge in our hearts and our physical bodies, eventually causing illness, pain and unhappiness. This is because true physical and emotional health comes only from living in the reality of God. We keep looking at these stories as if they are reality, reliving them over and over again. We make idols of them, worshiping them as if they are our true identity.

The Sufi path of healing shows us how to remove these veils from our heart, so that the truth is present. In that truth, peace, healing, mercy and all we are actually seeking emerges. We learn that God is present, not just during the good and easy times, but in hardship too. We learn to pay homage to all of the events of our lives. Love and certainty become unshakable inside our hearts. Therefore, even during the most difficult life events, we have the light of God to hold onto.

As part of my healing, I needed to remove my own veils. One of these veils was, "there is no place for me in the world." I started using the Sufi practices of Remembrance and receiving Sufi healing to clear out the memories and beliefs that held this veil in place. I first worked on the personal layer, which are the veils that came from my family life. There is no fault here. It is only the interpretation of life by a young child and the belief system that then formed.

I had always known that this was a core belief in my life. I had worked on it in psychotherapy. I had been a Buddhist practitioner, letting go of my thoughts. However, it was not until I started doing the Sufi practices and healings that the imprints of these memories left me completely. There were times as I practiced that I could feel light dissolving these memories from my heart and body, leaving me with "knowing" that God was holding me and there was a place for me here on earth. My health improved, my relationships improved and all I could see as I looked at my life was the thread of God's love moving through everything.

I am of Jewish heritage. The next layer of healing was to clear a collective belief of "there is no place for me in the world." This has been a theme of the Jewish people for centuries. As I brought the Sufi practices into the places in my body, heart and soul that continued to believe this story, I experienced visions of refugees tromping barefoot through the snow with no place to go. As I allowed myself to open these places to the light of God, the pictures dissolved. Modern epigenetics now tells us that historical experiences affect the DNA of future generations.

Healing sounds simple. Why would anyone want to hold onto veils that prevent us from living in the peace of God's love? But we believe our stories as the truth of who we are and fight to hold on. This is the inner jihad - the inner battle to surrender everything to be the servant of God versus the servant of our own beliefs and desires. In Sufism this is "to die before you die." Die to the story we have made up and that which we live.

As human beings we hold all the qualities of God inside of us. The qualities are like the warp and weft of a weaving. They form the tapestry of creation. Everything in creation is from God's qualities, and the human is the only one that holds them all. Much of healing comes from unraveling from our soul, a twisted understanding of each of these qualities so we can bring them to the world as God intended. We display compassion, but it is not as complete as God's compassion. We hold power, but we misuse it. Healing our understanding of the qualities is more than conceptual. As we walk the Sufi path, we are healing our distorted versions of these qualities and our whole being changes. We are now serving the world not from ourselves, but from God's light.

My body continues to be challenged by symptoms of physical illness, but I am certainly better than I was. My energy waxes and wanes. I use my pains and discomfort to bring me back to remembering God. This allows me to live a place inside that is deeper than any outer symptoms. As a result, my life has become richer and more full of love. I can say that my fear has been replaced with certainty, that my anger has been replaced by deep compassion and mercy and that I live more in surrender and service to God. Through the surrender of the veils, I have become more and more an instrument of His peace.

**Rahima Susan Schmall, Ph.D., R.N.**

Rahima Schmall, Ph.D., R.N. is a faculty member at USHS and department head of the Spiritual Healing and Counseling Department. She is a psychologist, registered nurse and master spiritual healer who has successfully blended spirituality, medical knowledge and modern psychology into her clinical practice and teaching for over thirty years. She is a former director of the Healing Intensive Retreat at the Shadhiliyya Sufi Center, as well as a former director of their "zawiyyah" or retreat program.

She has a deep love of God and is gifted at creating a safe and nurturing space in which people with physical illness or emotional pain can work through their issues to find peace, wholeness and harmony. As a teacher, she has a passion for helping each and every student develop their own unique gifts as a healer and human being. She has a private healing practice in which she helps people from all over the world find the healing that only comes through God's light.

# *Following Your Heart: A Story About One Man's Search for Healing and for God*

## Nur Al-Amin Preston

This story, my story, is a story about searching. This "search" that I am speaking of is actually something I believe is inside of all of us. The "search" could best be described as the feeling deep inside of us of going somewhere, being moved and being drawn. It's the feeling of looking for something we have not yet found, a deep inner longing.

This search and this longing is something that has propelled me throughout my life. I believe that it propels us all. It is a motion of seeking, learning and wanting. This longing is an inner music that can be heard. It is a music that I heard and was determined to follow.

My childhood life on the outside would be described as white suburban middle class. However, on the inside, it was one of deep depression, drug and alcohol addiction, suicide and despair.

My father was a deeply troubled, angry man, given to fits of rage and anger. He was an orphaned child who grew up in Oregon and moved to California to work in the casinos in Lake Tahoe.

My mother, for most of my young childhood, was also deeply unhappy. She left home at a very early age to become a professional ice skater. After a long series of events, she eventually met my father, and they got married. She and my father lived in South Lake Tahoe, California for some time, until the time came when my mother demanded they move.

My childhood home was put on the market, sold, and shortly after my 8th birthday, we packed up and moved down into the foothills of the mountains to a town called Shingle Springs.

Shortly after this move, our lives changed. My mother found the Church and Christianity. Overnight everything in our home changed, my mother changed and everything was pointed towards accepting Jesus.

It was a beautiful intention by my mother. However, it became living chaos in our home. My father and most of the family were against going to church. As insistent as my mother was that we go, my father was equally insistent that we not go.

I liked Church. I liked getting up and going to church every Sunday. I found the bible, invited Jesus into my heart through a Billy Graham Crusade and began to spend time every day reading and studying the religion.

Something else very notable happened to me at this time. Within days of inviting Jesus (peace be upon him) into my heart, I began to notice swings in my moods. A black depression began to creep into the crevices of my mind. As a child, I had always remembered being anxious, nervous, sensitive, and fearful. However, upon my conversion, these emotions took a dramatic turn.

At this time, I noticed something else inside of me. There was a longing, searching and knowing that peace and healing was out there somewhere. As a new Christian boy, I read in the New Testament Gospels of the bible, where Jesus (Isa), peace be upon him, says: "Come to Me all you who are weary, and rest. I will give you the drink in that you will never thirst again."

I was aware that, even with my newfound faith, I was still thirsty, and along with that thirst, I was in an enormous amount of physical and emotional pain.

The depression and darkness only worsened throughout my teenage years. My friends were all going out and having fun, going to parties, etc., but I could not make myself do that. When I was out with people, I felt alone and

I longed to be at home. I noticed a deep sadness taking over my life. It was becoming more and more pervasive. My sleep began to leave me for most of the night and when I did sleep, I would awake the next morning in utter terror with anxiety and fear overwhelming me.

Each day, I was beginning to force myself to live. My body felt heavy and, although I was an outstanding athlete in top shape, I always felt tired and distressed. I was never at peace.

I also noticed that I could not stop. As a teenager, I forced myself to work, play high school basketball and baseball and be in school. I was usually busy seven days a week. Inside I was feeling tremendous terror. I had the insight that if I stopped, the darkness would catch up to me.

With all of this going on, I turned to God. I asked God for healing and help, but nothing came. I longed for God and for the pain to leave my body and my soul. However, no matter how hard I tried, nothing came.

In the darkness, I knew there was light. In the darkest days of what would eventually be diagnosed as bi-polar depression, I knew that something was calling me. I knew that an answer was out there. I knew that there was a drink to drink where I would never thirst again.

As my high school experience continued, something inside me knew that I had to leave my home or death would certainly overtake me. I saw only one way out. I had a God-given talent for the game of baseball. Blessed with this gift in a family of non-athletes, I had always been something of a star. During my junior year of high school, it became apparent to me that this was my way out.

I gave myself over to practicing, working and getting better. I practiced day and night, and by my senior year, this began to pay off. I had a spectacular senior year. During one of my home games, my coach and I were approached by a scout from the University of California-Berkeley.

At that time, Berkeley had a budding Division 1 baseball program. Some

3 years later, they won the NCAA Division 1 World Series. They were the best Division 1 Team in the nation. As you can imagine, my coach and father were very excited. The scout asked me questions and then went on his way. In my heart, though, I knew that with my fragile state of mind, I could never survive at a school like Berkeley. My heart was drawing me to Los Angeles, where a friend of mine was attending the Master's College, a small private Christian school. This is what my heart was asking for.

Shortly after I discovered this, I informed my father and coach, who were both furious that I would turn down an opportunity like Berkeley. Too bad for them. I wrote a letter to the Coach at The Master's College stating my intentions and asked for a tryout.

The Master's College head coach, contacted my high school coach, and before I knew it, I was on my way to LA for a tryout. From the moment I stepped on the field for the tryout (I would be playing with the team in their summer league), something overtook me. I was not myself. I played as if I was in another dimension. I hit two home runs and combined that with a double. As a result, I was offered a modest scholarship and an open door.

For a brief time, I was happy. I came to Los Angeles and began my new life. I had new friends and was surrounded by a warm loving Christian environment of learning and experiencing my faith. Even my internal pain and restlessness began to subside and smooth out a bit.

This happiness would not last long. One fateful spring day, I was in the outfield fielding balls during batting practice. I was approached by my good friend and coach, who informed me that at the age of 58, my troubled father had died.

In that instant, the darkness descended on my heart like a wrecking ball. Everything I knew was somehow destroyed. As the details of my father's death began to emerge, our family found out that he was a victim of homicide. He was murdered.

Upon returning home from school that night, I sat at our kitchen table and began praying and asking God for help. I sat at our kitchen table searching my bible for an answer to the pain. I opened my bible and was led to the book of Job, the biblical story of pain. I read all of its 39 chapters that night. It was the story of a good man losing everything in this world. It was also the story of attempted trust and demand.

In the end of Job, after listening to the prattling of his friends, Job asks, or better said, demands, a meeting with God. God comes and answers him, showing him a glimpse of His Reality. The book ends with Job covering his mouth confessing his ignorance.

I sat at that table and looked in my heart. I found that I was not cursing God. I was not angry at God for what had happened in my life. I simply asked God for help. I asked God to show Himself to me. I longed and yearned for God. I asked God to relieve the pain, but in the moment and the years to come, it was not to be.

Over the next several years of my life, my longing and search for healing continued, and so did the pain. The depression got worse, and so did my life. I rarely slept, rarely ate, and my suffering got deeper. I asked God, begged God, searched the bible, the church, and many other things for healing, but nothing came.

Beyond the end of my rope, I turned to alcohol to give me respite. As one can imagine, one who suffers from bi-polar depression shouldn't drink, which was my case.

My drinking career, while short, had a devastating effect on my life. I saw my marriage of 17 years come to an end, and the investment advisory business that had been built from nothing also began to show cracks.

I was out of answers. Even worse, my will to live and keep searching was leaving me. During all these dark times, even my desire to get up every morning and pray, journal, read my bible and ask God to help was leaving me.

On a fateful night, I felt as if my life was over. I had spent that particular evening drinking even more than usual. I had gone into a place that was so dark, I knew I could not come back. As I headed from the bar to home, I had had enough. I sped my luxury car up to 155 MPH and recklessly drove it off the freeway, hoping that my longing would stop and so would the pain.

That was not to be so.

I crashed at 155 mph wearing no seat belt and with all the windows down. However, in the end, I woke up and much to my amazement, I was alive. The car was on fire, blood was pouring from my body, and everything was moving in slow motion, but I was alive.

I was sitting in the burning car and still feeling the determination to die. All of a sudden, I began to notice that it was quiet. Not quiet outside, for the metal was on fire and the engine was burning, but it was quiet...on the inside. The endless fear, grinding pain and desperation were all gone. I was at peace, and it was completely quiet. There was one other thing I noticed. Deposited in me at the moment from the angels I am sure, was a new desire to live and get better.

I woke up in the hospital the next morning and checked in with my heart. Yes, I still wanted to live. In that fateful car crash, God had taken my longing for death and replaced it with the longing for life. I no longer wanted to quit. I wanted to continue my search for what I knew was out there.

Even with my new found desire to live, I was still deeply sick. My body was exhausted from decades of unrest. I was still addicted to alcohol, my marriage was in ruins and my business was being taken from me. However, I wanted to live. I wanted to continue to search and to find the answer that I knew was out there.

I started to seek again in earnest. I began the wonderful life-saving program of AA. I saw new doctors and counselors. After many difficult nights of distress, I also began out of necessity to drop the religious beliefs I held so dearly. In this time, I left the path that I had loved for so many years behind.

I stepped back on the long dusty road and began to walk again.

With the alcohol gone, life began to get better, albeit slowly. I was still in enormous pain, but, somehow, I knew I was on the right path.

During this time in my life I was travelling back and forth between Los Angeles and Central America. I was going to Nicaragua, Costa Rica, and Panama, among other places. Along with the forms of recovery I was seeking, I found that being in this part of the world fed my heart and my body.

As I was preparing for one of my many trips down there, a friend of mine called me and asked to sit down for coffee. Since we had been friends for many years and he shared many of my current struggles, I agreed. We met at a local coffee shop on Saturday morning, where he asked me about the book, *The Power of Now,* by Eckhart Tolle.

I remembered that he had given me the book some months ago. I had read perhaps the first 10 pages or so, but thought it was not for me. I told him that I had the book, and he encouraged me to pick it up and give it another try.

I half-heartedly agreed. As I prepared to leave from LA, I put the book in my bag. On the way to the airport, I was led to take the book out and began to read it. As I was reading, I noticed that while my mind was telling me this was a waste, my heart found new life in the words I was reading. Between the initial flight, the connecting flight and layovers, I had about 16 hours to read and take in its message. I read the whole book on the flight. When I exited the plane in Costa Rica, I set my intention that during my stay there, I would practice living what I had just learned.

I was immediately put to the test. As I got off the plane and prepared to exit customs, the line was several hundred people long. I would probably be in that line just to get through customs for over two hours. As I looked over the sea of people, waiting to exit, I contemplated the mental options of trying to find an easier way, wanting to get frustrated, and again for some unknown reason, I decided to drop all those thoughts. I found myself, as the book taught, "in the present moment."

As I entered that space, I remember looking up at the ceiling of the airport. As I scanned the tile of the ceiling, I entered some other space that I cannot explain. In that space and in that moment, looking at the ceiling, the disease I called bi-polar, which I suffered with for over 30 years, left my chest and floated in one instant up through the ceiling of that airport.

I was in shock. I could not believe that just like that, it was gone. Yet, so it was. At this present point in my life some 8 years later, it has never returned. Just like that, it was gone......

Still in shock, the reality of God began to set in on me. I knew that God was out there. Not only was He out there, but He was listening to my prayers and responding.

With this experience and this amazing healing, I returned to Los Angeles a new man. I felt love flowing into my life. I saw the colors and felt the wind. I was alive, and, somehow, my search was almost over.

It was then that I was led to take my next step in faith. One night I found myself praying what I believe to be the most sincere prayer of my life. This prayer came from so deep inside of me that I know I could not have brought it there myself. It was very sincere and true.

I prayed: "Dear God, please let me hear Your voice."

That was it. I had reached the point where deep inside I needed to experience God, and not just know that He existed.

Soon after that, I was led to a local bookstore. It was a large, three-story bookstore. As I walked to the top floor, I was immediately transported to the back of the store. I stood in front a huge book shelf that would normally be filled with books, but not that day. As I stood in front of the huge book shelf, there was only one book. That book was called *A Course in Miracles*.

Convinced that I had received the next sign from God, I bought the book and began my new life. I read and read and read and began to learn of the inner world that I always knew existed. I learned of God and how to be connected deeply to Him, not through my mind as I had been trained, but through my heart.

I read the book night and day and began to practice what it taught me. I read 873 pages over a period of a few months and then...my prayer was answered.

I was in Orange County, CA, at my son's volleyball tournament. The tournament was played all day and into the evening. As I left the parking garage after it ended, I drove approximately six miles, and then heard a voice. The voice inside me simply said, "Go back." The voice was so shocking and clear that I obeyed it. I drove back to the parking garage and parked. I then heard the same voice say, "Go home." I drove the same six miles until I heard again, "Go back." This process repeated itself one more time. On the third time headed home, at the same place where I was asked to turn around, this time I heard in the clearest voice I have ever heard, "Your prayer has been answered. You have heard My voice, and you have passed the test."

I was in awe and felt the warmth of hope begin to come in. I could feel my yearning for my search to find healing and God multiply.

I checked inside and still I had not found what I was searching for. My longing continued.

One fateful night when I was attending a meeting in North Hollywood, CA, a friend of mine who knew of my struggles with depression came up to me and said that she had a session with a Sufi healer, and she recommended that I go and see her.

Even with my new found experiences with healing and God, my personal life was in shambles with my marriage over and my business coming apart. Therefore, my heart jumped at the possibility of help. I agreed and scheduled an appointment with the Sufi Healer the next week.

I did not know what to expect at the appointment. I did not know even what a Sufi healing was. My friend, whom I trusted, recommended that I go, and so I did. When I sat down in this person's living room, she explained the healing process. It was basically identifying what issue or problem in my life I wanted to work on, and then taking that issue into a process where the healer prayed these "special" prayers in Arabic, and as she explained it, connected us to the Light.

Being a bit wary, she asked me if I was comfortable with her using the Arabic language and the name for God, Allah. Due to my Christian upbringing, on any other day, this would perhaps have been offensive to me, but, again, my heart answered for me and we proceeded.

That healing, and the proceeding ones that I received over the next few months, along with the exercises the healer gave me to do, was unlike anything I had ever experienced. Not only did the healing bring relief and comfort, but I felt like the door was opening for my search to be over. I felt a drawing, a pulling if you will, that allowed me to let go and just surrender to it. Somehow, deep inside I knew that I was experiencing God, the Truth.

At that time, the healer mentioned that there was a school where I could go and learn the ways of the Sufi healer. This place was called The University of Spiritual Healing and Sufism, located in Northern California.

This was a big break from everything that I had done in my life. Up to this point, I was a very successful investment advisor having built a small firm from nothing, and was living very well. However my marriage of 17 years had come to a close, my business was in shambles, and I had felt that life as I knew it was slipping away.

In the process of signing up for Sufi School, a friend of mine mentioned a workshop that was taking place up in Northern California, called the Path of Love. My heart immediately opened to the workshop, and I set my intention to go. The workshop was going to be held starting on Friday night, and as it turns out that was the only night I could attend.

I drove the six hours up to Palo Alto, CA, and parked in a dark school parking lot. I had to walk up a long hill to get to the home where the workshop was being held. I was feeling a bit timid, wondering why I had driven all this way to go to this workshop and meet this guy, Sidi.

When I opened the door to come in, my anxiety grew. I was a Christian white boy in the middle of people dressed in hijab and turbans, the traditional clothing of the Muslim's and the Sufis. I was taken aback. I held very tightly to my Christian roots. Although I knew that path did not work for me any longer, when I walked in that door I just wanted to turn around and leave.

However, I noticed that my heart did not want to leave. I noticed the pull inside me drawing me closer.

Therefore, despite all my feelings, I walked in and sat down. The individual hosting the weekend introduced the program, and then I was instructed to go downstairs for the newcomers program. This was being taught by Dr. Wadude Laird and his wonderful wife Nura. I sat down and began to take in the class and listen to the beautiful sounds of "La illaha illa 'llah." This chant, the vibration, the feel and the music of this chant was unlike anything I had ever experienced. Everything in me opened, as I felt the pure love of God flow into me.

Saying that chant, feeling it in my chest and smelling its scent, I knew that I was again experiencing God. I knew I was close.

From then on, I was sold on going to the University and signed up to join the April 2013 class.

When the time to attend school came, I began the long drive from Los Angeles to where the school was being held in Pope Valley, CA, just outside of the Napa Valley. The drive was difficult, and the school was hard to find. I arrived not only frustrated, but I was in serious doubt as to whether this was the place for me or not.

Once again, when I arrived and got out of the car, I was faced with the same picture of women and men in traditional Muslim clothing. Once again, everything in me was saying to turn around and go home.

As I stood in front of my car, figuring out all the reasons I had to turn and leave, I was given the gift I had been looking for all my life.

The local Iman was walking up the porch to a PA system. He stood there for a moment, turning on the microphone system and was getting ready to give me my gift from the Hands of God.

As the Iman put the microphone up to his mouth, he began to sing this song. It was a prayer really, a calling. I did not know what this calling was in the moment, since all I could do was sit there and listen. I was awestruck as a lifetime of struggle and pain dissolved. Those beautiful words dropped deep inside me one by one, leading me to the place where I always called "home."

In that moment, my heart drank, and drank, and drank and then drank some more. My heart took in everything in that moment, and when that prayer (which Muslim's and Sufi's both call the Adan, the Muslim call to prayer) was done, I was weeping, crying and I was home. My search was over. I walked into my new home.

My beloved Guide, Sidi Al-Jamal, may Allah bless his secret and raise his station before Him, always would tell us in his words to "take our chance." He would tell us in his teachings that the doors were open, and to leave everything behind and walk through. He would tell us to follow the pathway of our Heart.

May God bless all of you in your search, and give you knowing that it is not in vain. As Jesus (Isa), peace be upon him, was recorded saying, "Knock and the door will be opened to you." Keep searching, keep knocking and follow your heart.

## Nur Al-Amin Preston

Nur Jeffrey Preston currently serves as a member of the Enrollment Team at the University of Spiritual Healing and Sufism, where he is also finishing his Masters of Divinity in Peacemaking. Nur holds a Bachelor's Degree in Psychology from The Master's College in Los Angeles, California.

Nur has been a spiritual seeker for over 35 years, and a student of Sufism for 3 years. Nur's lifetime commitment to seeking and living the truth eventually led him to study with Shaykh Sidi Al-Jamal of Jerusalem, where he has found clarity and a deep connection to God.

Nur and his family live in Southern California, where he is a community leader and runs a successful spiritual healing practice. Nur helps individuals suffering from various forms of mental and emotional illnesses to bring healing, peace and harmony to their lives and the lives of their families.

# *Mercy Beyond Explanation*

## Sukayna Ronda Mau, MA, LPC

Mercy beyond explanation,

Healing beyond hopes,

Longings met with unfolding answers beyond the limits of time,

Family beyond simple human connection,

Understandings beyond doctrine,

Life beyond day to day existence,

Certainty beyond identified beliefs,

Map beyond any known territory,

Reality beyond words & mental comprehension,

Love beyond love,

Gratitude far beyond prediction.

—*Sukayna Ronda Mau, MA, LPC*

The memory has always stayed with me. I stood in my front yard, gazing over the roof of our family home up into the limitless cyan sky. I continued my 8-year-old ponderings during the walk home from school that day. I wondered how I could know for sure what was real. This was a burning question for me. I was not terribly fond of this life, what it meant to be me trying to navigate the mysteries of this world. Even back then, without anyone really telling me, I had an awareness that birth was not my beginning. I just could not figure out what I had done wrong to get kicked out of where I came from and sent into this dense, challenging realm.

I found myself influenced by strong fears in the culture at the time (of Communists, Martians, etc.) and even wondered if my parents were who they appeared to be. In those moments of reflection, the only conclusion I could find was that my imagination is what I could know for sure was real. If nothing in the world was as it seemed, something had to be making it all up. Realizing that, I experienced a profound sense of separation from everyone and everything. The only exception was my sure awareness of the Source of it all, maybe what others referred to as God? For as long as I can remember, there has always been a very strong longing to bridge "Home" with here and discover the purpose of being incarnated into such a world and life as this.

During the following four and a half decades, I continued to ponder and become a seeker of Truth that resonated within my flood of questions. I tasted many paths in hopes of discovery of where I might fit. Along the way I tried the teachings of Yogananda, Buddhism, Contemplative Prayer, the Unity Church, Taoism, and various flavors of Christianity. I learned things from each and every approach. Christianity and Jesus became very dear to my heart. The Christian culture and the focus on doctrine, though, often left me with more questions and my hunger for the way home not met. I witnessed many times where the culture deviated from the held doctrine and teachings in the Bible, which confused me. I also felt the intense pressure to look and be good in order to be culturally acceptable, so my sense of isolation remained and maybe even grew a little.

I realized that one of my deep values was to be honest and authentic, but where was the freedom to be me without judgements waiting? Was this another place where I was going to get kicked out? This is not at all a perspective of blame, but rather the very things I struggled with (a feeling of isolation and questions with no apparent answers) was mirrored back to me well. I spent three years in Bible college, hoping to break this spell. I discovered many, many gifts in my stay in Christendom, but could not find the keys to unlock the doors for what I most desperately sought: a way to deeply connect with God and a community to do the spiritual journey with, where I felt I could belong. I realized that I required wise help, so I began to pray for a teacher sent by God, to help me discover what I had been searching for.

In 2004, I discovered the wrapped treasure of a teacher. Sidi, whom we refer to as our teacher and guide (and turned out was God's answer to my prayer for a teacher), was different than anyone I had ever met. I was skeptical, and then timid, about accepting what would be revealed to me in a progressive unfolding that has now become the ground on which I rest my seeking. To be clear, I am definitely, after almost 13 years on the Sufi path, still feeling like I am just beginning to learn to walk to my true Home, finding my way through the thicket of this world to the discoveries of what is Real. I do now hold a certainty that this is the path designed by my Creator that best fits me personally to do so. I am very grateful that my deepest longings did not go unheard, even when I was not sure how to hold them any longer for myself.

My humanity trips me up almost continually, but I cannot give up because I am unable to deny the gift of this path that functions to unveil me. It takes my breath away with discoveries. When I ponder now, my heart often feels like it will burst trying to contain all of the humble excitement of dreams being realized. My belief, of which I had come to embrace as almost certainly true, "I will never really belong anywhere" has vanished without my mind really knowing how, except to know God heard my cry and met me there with grace.

It all began in such an unexpected setting. After professionally being in the psychotherapy field for almost 20 years, I had become accustomed to attending continuing education and personal development seminars. I carried a mix of curiosity and reserved judgement about new practical discoveries that could move my clients and myself forward on our healing & growth journeys regarding age-old issues. While having dinner with a friend and colleague on a summer evening in 2004, she shared with me about a training she had attended weeks before. She reported having as deep of an experience with the taught process in the seminar as she had come across in any other training for the last two decades. She was then quite direct with me, telling me I HAD to take this training. I was known in my professional circles as being a "workshop junkie" (yep, still seeking), so I thought nothing of her request and signed up for the next convenient offering. When I walked through the door that day, little did I know that it was far more than a threshold into a conference room of just another training session. I know now it was a doorway into places, previously unknown to me, in my own heart that led to passageways of the Reality that I had spent my life seeking. It both invited me to choose what steps I wanted to take, while also almost knowing what I would choose, and moved me like a current in a stream towards my heart's Home. The question for the first few years was, "Is this a way I can trust?"

Just one month after this first exposure to Sufism, I found myself attending my first session of a three-year program that we now know as The University of Spiritual Healing and Sufism. I did not yet know why I was really there. I just knew I wanted to experience more of what began happening in me, and my awareness, with the introductory weekend workshop. I am not one to jump into anything quickly, and I was a bit freaked out by them calling God "Allah" and the inferences to Islam. There was an intense hesitancy about the outer dressings, but I was not able to deny what was blossoming in my own heart. I sat in the back, kept silent and observed just about everything to try and understand what it was about this mysterious, uncomfortable path that was undeniably attracting me. Sidi taught in those days almost solely about Jesus, or so it seemed to me. This opened a connection of safety between Jesus, Sidi's heart and my own. I loved what he taught and it was perfectly in alignment with what I had experienced in my Christian worship, except the doctrine about Jesus being God incarnate. Sidi did not focus, thankfully, on that at all.

After enough time passed to see the clear connection between Sufism and Islam, I had a heart to heart with my Executive Director (what I have at times called God). All I could find to say was, "You have got to be kidding!!! You could not have picked a more challenging path for me. I am extremely uncomfortable with Your Arabic name. Everyone in my family and circle of friends may leave and think I have abandoned You for a group of terrorists. How will I ever use anything I learn here to help my clients? Are You sure this is what You want for me? I am scared I will be cast out yet again." I felt like a place where two trains had collided head on at full speed. My mind did not like it at all, but I felt compelled to discover what was happening deeper inside of me. I was opening the cracked door to discover that which I had been seeking was waiting for me.

Twelve and a half years later, there are still no words to adequately describe what has happened to and for me, but I do know Who has happened. The feelings of isolation and shame, that I did something bad enough to get kicked out, still tries to ring my doorbell. However, rarely do I answer their request to enter. In the moments I experience God's compassion and love, and willingness to never let go, I know I am Home. The Sufi community, which I have such a privilege and joy to journey and serve with, is full of folks whose souls speak a language my soul knows more deeply than any other. It turns out that the values and focus are almost opposite of what I feared in the beginning. I smile at the miracle in my neuropathways that God, Who goes by many names, including Allah, has become a place of rest and peace in my being. The key for me was that I did not quit and let the old beliefs (about not being worth keeping instead of being kicked out, isolated, alone, and a world where nothing could be known with certainty to be real) override my seeking and finding. Sidi tells us over and over to, "Don't stop because there is so much more." I am so grateful my human judgments and fears did not own me and my heart continued to travel on.

Except for a short break because of family needs, since graduation I have continued to learn and serve at the Sufi university filled with sacred opportunities to come alongside students and faculty alike. It keeps me humble in the stream's current that moves us all forward through the stations of spiritual development and deepening. I know the whole university team of servants, as well as many of the members of the community across the country and globe. They dedicate themselves to carrying the message of Peace, Love,

Mercy, Justice and Freedom that Sidi instructed us to live by and share with any seeking heart. I could not ask for a more desirable people to journey alongside. No one is perfect or walks on water. We are all very human and each of us is guilty of acting out of our shadow side at times. What I have come to treasure though, is each of us is seeking to know God. We seek Allah's help to heal our own shadow to not miss our chance to glimpse into the Holy Jewel (the secret He has hidden in every soul for our discovery) that lives in each of us and is the truth of our existence and purpose. I have discovered the people and situations in my life mirror my fears, doubt, ego and my story (that which veils my inner Reality) that I may more clearly see where I need Allah's mercy and healing. When I remember Allah, and choose to trust, everyone who challenges me becomes my teacher. It is not always easy, but it is worth the progress it brings in me. I am left with states of gratitude over and over.

What I have learned from USHS, Sidi's books and teachings and the Qur'an has not only changed my experience, but has significantly transformed my counseling practice. God has blessed me with clients and students from many varied backgrounds and faiths. I see myself as someone who is called to come alongside of them, honoring how the "Executive Director" is leading their journey. When I am specifically guided and secure permission, I utilize the Sufi healing protocols that Sidi has taught us. What I have been amazed by, after over 30 years in the counseling field, is that there is little out there I have found more helpful and effective than the Sufi healing process, not only from my perspective, but also by reports of both clients and students.

To share one amazing miracle of how a client experienced the power of Allah's healing, I share, with her permission, a story of a woman who struggled for decades with an extreme flying phobia. She had flown to Europe with a family member during the previous twenty-four hours and reported the energy of the flying phobia whispered no threatening thoughts or suggestions of extreme action in order to survive on her trip. It had mysteriously vanished! No medications were needed and she was even able to sleep on the flight. We had a session just the day before she left, and my plan for the past several weeks was to address this phobia. I have had a track record with a number of clients over the years to greatly diminish this fear with a specific protocol. The plan though, was derailed by the critical injuries her only sibling sustained in an accident a few weeks earlier, ending with death just days before our session. Einstein's teachings about, "The significant problems we face today cannot be solved at the same level of thinking we were at when we created them" is something, as a therapist, I have always kept in my awareness. This client's resource state to address the flying phobia problem state was understandably very depleted. I decided not to add to it by addressing the phobia head on, but rather to end our time with a Sufi Light Prayer. I translated each line in the prayer after reciting it in Arabic and waited for the imagination to help use the senses to be aware of Allah's saturating Light delivery.

When she returned from her travels, also being free from her fears on the return trip, I asked her what she attributed the shift to. In her words she said, "I think it was that Sufi thing you did." Honestly, that caught me by surprise, for it was purposed in my heart as a gentle blessing dealing with her grief, with no intentional focus for it to affect the flying phobia. Once again, Allah was answering far beyond all I could hope or conceive. She has asked to do some version of the Light Prayer in most sessions since.

My heart and faith were deeply affected by this experience. I continue to open understandings about other healing protocols taught at USHS and Sidi's talks as well. Insights into divine intentions for our healing and how that interfaces with faith are such a gift. We use the word "walking" to refer to our spiritual journey and its practices. Sidi always told us that "the healing was in the walking, and the walking was in the healing". Healing is so much more than feeling better, although some are content to stop there. The process of healing reveals in its uncovering so many holy secrets if we take our chance and have eyes and ears to be awake. I have come to know that there is no situation where this is not true. The biggest secret is the gift Allah hid deep in each of our beings, our heart of hearts, that we may discover the realities of Reality. Illusions and stories are no longer relevant there. The reality of you and the reality of you in the Divine Presence is what is left. The things I have longed and looked for my whole life are as dim reflections in the mirror of what has also been longing for me.

Here is a tasting of one version of The Light Prayer through the Divine Qualities in English. Please note that I am so grateful for the Arabic, and there are ways for you to get the Arabic phrase for each line. Contact me if you are interested.

*Oh Allah! Oh Merciful! Grant me Light in my heart!*
*Oh Allah! Oh Compassionate! Grant me Light in my hearing!*
*Oh Allah! Oh Sovereign Lord! Grant me Light in my sight!*
*Oh Allah! Oh Holy! Grant me Light from above me!*
*Oh Allah! Oh Giver of Peace! Grant me Light from beneath me!*
*Oh Allah! Oh Giver of Faith! Grant me Light from my right side!*
*Oh Allah! Oh Guardian! Grant me Light from my left side!*
*Oh Allah! Oh Majestic! Grant me Light in front of me!*
*Oh Allah! Oh Compeller! Grant me Light from behind me!*
*Oh Allah! Oh Superb! Grant me Light in my whole self!*
*Oh Allah! Oh Creator! Bestow Light in my home!*
*Oh Allah! Oh Shaper from naught! Bestow Light in my children's hearts!*
*Oh Allah! Oh Fashioner! Bestow Light in my homeland!*

As I mentioned earlier, I choose to proceed slowly with each line until I experience each part of my being overflowing with Light to the point of saturation, where no darkness remains outside of illumination. I do not choose to manipulate the process in any way, but choose to trust the intelligence of the Light. I do set my focus on facing the Light, with courageous honesty of what I am experiencing in that moment, and letting it clean me the same way I stand beneath the water in the shower. This Light though, is not blocked by skin or boundaries of any sort. I say "Yes!" to it overflowing within every atom and atomic sub-particle of my physical body, my spiritual self to the fullest extent of its existence, my thoughts and emotional self, and all the interconnections of my relationships. In those moments, I experience, beyond comprehension, the prayer as healing and quieting the sources of my pain and self-management. I am able to allow the Light to do and bring what It has for me. It feels like a miracle because my mind is not fully able to go where it takes me.

Over the decades, I have studied and been certified in many approaches to counseling and healing. Many of them were considered to be cutting edge. I am impressed that there are similarities between what some of my professional training has offered and the ones I have continued to learn at USHS. However, I had not experienced any that left silence where white noise and chaos had previously lived, until I found Sufism. Only in walking this path have I felt undeniable breakthroughs for myself. I am still pondering what it is that happens, for the finite mind cannot easily identify the power and effects of an encounter with the Infinite Eternal.

The Sufi Path is about returning, not only to a place of connection, but to what we refer to as the Unity. It is the place that can witness the Infinite Reality beyond story, or doctrine, or definition, or adequate description, and true Peace becomes breath. It is similar for me as love. No one can really help us comprehend love until we experience love by fully surrendering into it. The effects of trauma are one of many veils that keeps us from this place of witnessing what is Real, now and in Eternity. Bringing the age old Divine Sufi Wisdom to the effects of trauma, and being human, is the work to which I surrender to Allah's calling, in myself and in service to others.

My journey with Allah has just begun, and I experience a Niagara Falls of gratitude repeatedly. It is beyond what I was seeking and hoped for. It is far, far beyond. I have found Home.

## Sukayna Ronda Mau, MA, LPC

Sukayna (Ronda) Mau is a Licensed Professional Counselor near Portland, Oregon. Her work, which spans over three decades, began with designing and coordinating a referral program, coordinating between the juvenile court and two school districts, to identify and come alongside at-risk youth. Programs for the middle and high school girls were run in and out of the school settings and included training many volunteers to offer support and a point of contact for them. She also served as staff in a group home for girls who were no longer able to live at home with their parents.

Later, after finishing a graduate program at Lewis & Clark College, she transitioned into a full-time counseling practice addressing primarily trauma recovery. She has been trained and certified in many Energy Psychology approaches, including HBLU, AIT, NET, NLP, EMDR, Energy Medicine, EFT, and TFT. Sukayna also has served as a state-certified clinical supervisor for therapists looking to become licensed. For two years, she was the school counselor for a private Muslim school, with students in preschool through the 12th grade, near Portland, Oregon.

In 2004, Sukayna found herself in a weekend seminar that taught healing through the teachings of Sufism. She attended what is now known as The University of Spiritual Healing and Sufism. She completed the program, including the academic portion of the Masters in Ministry. Since graduating in 2007, except for 2 years off for family reasons, Sukayna has served both students and faculty in her responsibilities as a TA and Lead TA at USHS. She has taken some service responsibilities in her local Sufi community and is also on the USHS Board's alumni committee.

At home, Sukayna is a widowed mother of two and a grandmother of four. Her home has been a place for retreat, teachings, counseling, and support for many, but most of all, a heart that longs for God.

# *Fighting Every Step of the Way*
# Maryam Thea Elijah, M.Ac.

I grew up in a household that had many different spiritual paths represented. It wasn't my biological family but I spent most of my childhood in the home of a man named Lex Hixon, or Sheik Nur al-Jerrahi. In the Hixon household, there were always dervishes in the living room and Hindus in the basement. There were also Reclamation rabbis at the kitchen table and Eastern orthodox priests sitting around in the library. It was a house filled with serious religious practitioners of many different paths, all of whom were immersed in interfaith dialogue and had a deep understanding of the Unity. They were also the kind of people who were genuinely interested in having a conversation with an 8-year-old child about the nature of truth, beauty or anything else. They truly wanted to know what I thought.

I grew up having incredible conversations at the breakfast table. I played hide and seek and would pop out to find somebody translating Ramprasad's hymns to Kali, and read them to me. There was tremendous richness of spiritual treasure all around me as I grew up. Even though I loved all of it and felt very comfortable with all of it, I did not feel that there was one of those paths that was my own. Lex was a Sheik and a spiritual guide for many people. However, to me he was more like Papa. He was someone on whose lap I would sit and pull on his hair or something. He was not my Sheik. He was a huge influence, but more like a father's influence.

As I got older, I was a great explorer of spiritual paths and a great explorer of what you might call altered, perfected or expanded states of consciousness, lucid dreaming, Shamanic this and that... I never went the drug route. I figured

I was weird enough already, and that I could do this without stimulants of that sort. I was definitely an explorer and it was not really like any one place was my route or my home. I had graduated from acupuncture school and a classmate named Greg Lee handed me a flier for an Ibrahim Jaffe workshop, saying, "I think you should go to this. I'll pay for it, and if you think it was worthwhile, you can pay me back. Otherwise, it's fine."

It turned out that I couldn't go to the workshop because I wasn't free that weekend. However, there was a gathering that was happening afterwards in somebody's living room, where about 15 or so people were sitting around on the floor of this living room with Ibrahim. He told everybody the truth about themselves, right to their face, with so much love and compassion that no one felt ashamed. It was absolutely astounding. I was completely blown away by it. At that moment, I thought that was love with 4-wheel drive. I wanted to learn whatever he has learned to be able to tell the truth like that, and have it be okay to speak the truth.

Not that everybody got it right away. With a tight jaw, they might say, "What do you mean I'm holding anger at my father?" Everybody in the room could see that what Ibrahim was saying was totally true, yet the person couldn't see it. Then about 20 minutes later, their whole body would relax and be like, "oh, got it." Of course, the same thing happened to me. He said something completely outrageous. I don't even remember what it was, and thought, "no way, what do you mean?" I didn't feel ashamed. I didn't feel anything negative. I just didn't get it yet. Then at a certain point it hit me, and I said, "oh my gosh, unbelievable!"

At this point, I felt so vulnerable that I hated him. It was a thought or feeling process something like, "Ok you got me, now you have to die!" It was such an amazingly violent emotion. I have to say I didn't, at that time, think of myself as an intensely hostile and emotionally violent person. I learned through the Sufi path the degree to which I really was a seething hell pit of dominance ploys, resentment and power struggles. But I didn't know that at the time. This was my first eruption into, "You just touched my heart; I'll have to kill you now."

I was so impressed by how incredibly well Ibrahim handled it. He did it without being rocked by it whatsoever. He wasn't flustered or threatened by it at all. He was simply presencing, "Someone who's just been touched is now throwing fire my way. Okay beloved, what's going on in your heart?" I was very impressed by that. I really didn't want to kill him. I just couldn't handle my own vulnerability. He turned to see what was bothering me so much. I don't know exactly what he did, but it helped me clear something that allowed me to breathe very differently. I was able to just deal with the truth. It was a huge healing.

At the end of that session. Ibrahim said to me, "So, are you ready to take the promise?" I said a lot of dithering things like, "I need to think about it. I need to know more about it..." I gave a whole bunch of temporising objections. I really do understand from a certain perspective how what Ibrahim did next could look really bad. All I can say is that if what he did next hadn't been okay, I would have felt that, and I would have been very angry. This actually wasn't bad. It was completely accurate and right on. That's why it was okay.

He took my hands and in the midst of my objections said to me, "Repeat after me: I promise you Allah..." I started taking the promise and started to sob very hard. It was huge massive sobbing. It was lifetimes, generations, and aeon's worth of sobbing and sobbing coming up out of me as I took the promise. It was incoherent. Then at a certain point, I stopped sobbing and started laughing uncontrollably, with huge tears streaming down my face. I couldn't breathe. Salima started laughing and other people started laughing. Salima said, "I no longer feel mad that I missed my dhikr tonight; here is my dhikr." I just couldn't stop laughing.

It then switched to sobbing again. I sobbed and sobbed. I actually still have a little blue glass container of the tissues from blowing my nose and wiping my eyes from those tears. It was because they felt like the holiest tears of my life.

I then went my way and somehow or other, my contact information didn't connect. I guess because it was the end of the day and I was the only one taking the promise. As a result, nobody took my contact information or got back to me about anything. That's why a full 6 months went by and I had no idea what I had just done. However, I sure was feeling it reverberate. I was changed for life with no map and no explanation. So much of what I had previously been involved in, I wasn't even interested in anymore. These new ways had opened, and I was blown open without knowing any of the details of what it meant.

I'm actually very grateful that it happened that way. It gave me six months to feel in my body what it meant to take the promise, without having anything cognitive around it that I could object to. It was a purely experiential event. Thank goodness, because eventually after about 6 months, I thought to myself, "Hey, I think it's time for me to find out more about this. Who is this man, Ibrahim, and what else goes on here?"

I went to a basic introductory workshop with Ibrahim in Austin, Texas. It was a dramatic event in itself. I received the name Maryam, which I initially objected to thoroughly. I said, "You're naming me after a virgin? You've got to be kidding." My self-image of Maryam did not fit even slightly. Now that I am a mother, I understand myself and I understand Maryam differently. It's a perfect name.

The whole notion of Islam was difficult for me because I'm Jewish. My family has a very anti-Arab perspective. Arabs, I was taught, are the ancient enemy. They want to turn the seas red with our blood. It's a matter of extermination, them or us. There is not and never will be peace. It was a tremendous prejudice. Therefore, it was very difficult for me at first to say the word "Allah". For a year, I wouldn't say Allah. I would say Elohim or Adonai or whatever I could think of at that time. The change came when I was trying to pray and was sobbing at the same time. Allah is definitely the easiest name of God to say while you are sobbing. It struck me as extremely practical to have a name of God to call upon when you need it most.

I went to the healing school which is now USHS. I disliked almost everything about it. I didn't like that the moment I got there, I no longer felt special because of being smart. That really bothered me tremendously. It bothered me that the teachers were not academic, scholarly or intellectual. It bothered me that they talked in very simple language and wanted me to feel things in my body. I had no idea what they even meant by that. It made me mad that we had to lie on the floor and feel some energy somewhere and transform it. I felt nothing. It filled me with distrust that Ibrahim would say wildly inaccurate things, from a scholar's perspective.

For instance, Ibrahim once said something about Noah and his 4 sons. Hey, Noah had three sons and their names were Ham, Shem and Japheth. Do you seriously expect me to entrust the well-being and guidance of my soul to a man who thinks Noah had 4 sons? The answer in the long run is yes, because who the heck really cares whether Noah has 3 or 4 sons? I understand where I was coming from back then. There was a notion of rigour that shaped my notion of what safety actually consists of. That level of intellectual rigour was rarely manifest in the teachers that I was working with. It turned out in the long run that there was a wholly different kind of rigour at work. That other rigour was more important for the guidance of my soul and for the care of my heart.

For instance, I noticed that all of the teachers and the TAs were scrupulous in keeping the door of their heart open, even when I was unbelievably hostile and obnoxious towards them. There was this feeling of a door with a very specific frame. The message was that the door is always open, and I'd have to put down my weapons to get through it. For a long time, I wasn't willing to put down my weapons. They were mostly my intellectual weapons. This was because I didn't feel safe without them. I didn't know that there was another level of discernment by which I could know that I could trust this. It eventually became clear that they really meant it—that love is what they were aligned with—that there was truth that was not intellectual truth—that it could include intellectual truth, but only when that intellectual truth was fully transparent and integral to the love.

The teachings around love and truth probably were the most influential in helping me not fight the basic premise that this was safe and okay. I eventually accumulated enough examples of truth and love being identical. There is really no such thing as one existing without the other. In other words, if it's not truthful, it's not the real love and if it's not loving, it's not the real truth. Once I'd been around and around with that with the teachers enough times, I understood that there was an impressive rigour at work. It was, in fact, the rigour that led me to being drawn to Ibrahim. He had the ability to speak truthfully with love, so that it could be heard without shame.

That's probably Chapter One. It involved the big fight that I came through, to embracing Allah as the way of both love and truth. However, there were many other things that I fought along the way. For instance, the whole notion of the role of women, or even what it means to be a woman. That was huge. I was raised by a pro-ERA feminist mother. She was an attorney with a quick mouth. Nobody could get away with any sexist bullshit in front of her without getting a whole courtroom descending upon them. She could speak out and speak up. I was very proud of her for that. She raised me as a feminist. She raised me to think of myself as equal to any man, with a tremendous sense of strength.

Her image of womanhood, I later came to understand through Islam, was an image of womanhood predicated on men being totally clueless selfish jerks. The basic perspective was: if men are going to be clueless selfish jerks, here is what a woman is going to need to do. What I began to understand through Islam, by gaining an understanding of masculinity and femininity in relation to each other, is that if men are not being clueless selfish jerks and they are fulfilling the role of their manhood with decency, honour and nobility—then what it could mean to be a woman is very different and that it might be safe to be soft. It might be safe to trust and to yield. When a man has in his heart the well-being of my heart as a deep holy jewel as his primary intention, I am safe with him. If a man is being truly aware and respectful of my essence, then to surrender to him feels wonderful. Understanding this felt like the opening of a door to a dimension that I didn't even know was within me. For the first time, through the Islamic understanding of womanhood, I was feeling safe enough to discover that a woman is infinity unfolding in kaleidoscopic bliss.

I didn't know that about myself. I thought I was a fighter. And yet there was this whole world of richness inside of me that I hadn't even suspected. It was like a secret garden or an ocean of jewels. It was so beautiful and so infinite. All of this is treasure that can only be shared in the deepest state of trust and surrender. I just didn't know. My feminist mother, also a fighter, couldn't teach me because she didn't know either. I thank my feminist mother for carving out the space for me in the outer world, and for taking the first step in making me understand I am not made for subjugation. Islam then helped me take the next step, which is to understand that there is a very big difference between subjugation and surrender.

Speaking of which, I was certainly triggered at first, and objected strenuously to, the notion of being considered the slave of Allah. The whole notion of slave-hood was abominable to me as an American obsessed with the notion of freedom. The word slave was about the most horrible word there could be. It was obvious that this was partially based on the American history of having done such terrible things to African-American people in this country. But it was also the most horrible word just because, if freedom is the ideal, a slave is the worst thing to be. I definitely wanted freedom very much. I was willing to fight for it.

It took a long time to understand that freedom is not really worth all that much. It's kind of like Walmart, where you have all these different choices. It makes you feel really free, but what good is freedom without quality? What's that for? How many types of chewing gum do you need to feel like you're free?

This understanding took a long time to come. It took a lot of experimentation with the whole notion of guidance. What is guidance? Why would I follow guidance? Why is striving to receive clear guidance so much more valuable than striving for freedom? It took a long time to understand this on different levels—and I initially fought them all.

First, there is guidance on the level of the teacher or the guide telling me something, and me not being really willing to hear it. I can't tell you about how many times I was with Sidi in those first years, usually in Salima's house, asking him some questions about Chinese medicine. He would shout at me, "Maryam, do not stop with the outside picture!" He was thundering and hollering, and it was so intense that I would just crawl out of the room and shake in the corner for half an hour. Then I'd pull myself back together and come right back in, and ask yet another question, something argumentative and challenging, and he would thunder at me again—and I would go out of the room and shake and then come right back at it.

One of the really wonderful things I learned about not accepting Sidi's guidance, is that you don't die as a result. This was great to know! I learned that I did have free will at that level, and I could recover and come back again and he would be right there. I learned the same thing from the teachers. If I wasn't going to follow their guidance, they would kind of shrug and wait. I really appreciated that. I have free will. I can accept the guidance or not accept the guidance.

I got more and more effectively worked over in the program. I started having some sort of guidance coming through me and I was able to discern the different voices. Since I was very stubborn, there was still guidance that I didn't follow. This was even if it was coming through me, because I wanted what I wanted. If I really wanted what I wanted, then I didn't care if Allah wanted something else. Over time, I did a great many experiments with doing what I wanted instead of doing what Allah wanted. The pattern of results became pretty clear in the long run.

I remember the day in which it finally occurred to me what was going on. I said to myself, "Oh, if Allah wants something for me, *it's because that's best for me*." Somehow, that had not sunk into me before. It was because I was too busy with freedom and trying to get what I wanted. It slowly became more and more evident that if Allah wanted something for me, it was because it was really a good idea. If Allah did not want me to do something, it was because it really wasn't a good idea, no matter how much I thought I wanted it. That's when the whole notion of obedience began to seem like a more sensible option. My understanding of slave-hood became an understanding of taking my own free will and getting into a guidance groove so deep that I didn't have to think twice if I was going to do it or not.

I would definitely not say that I have, at this point, achieved slave-hood. I would say that I have a certain intermittency around degrees of independence. When I'm doing really well, I do not feel like an independent organism. I do not feel as though my thoughts are being thought by me, nor that my emotions are being felt by me. They are sort of being felt by me plus. Slave-hood is me in the groove, me and the guidance moving together. There is no clear decision point between myself and the guidance that I'm flowing with. Thus, I came to see slave-hood as an ideal rather than an abomination.

There were a number of Sufi practices that seemed ridiculous, such as writing the stations. I thought that was the stupidest thing ever. It was *Music of the Soul*, the section on the 28 Stations, which made absolutely no sense to my scholarly, intellectual mind. These writings were gibberish and were the ravings of a mad man. I had no idea what he was talking about. They also all seemed very repetitive. I rebelled intellectually by thinking, "There is no information contained in this. I don't get it. I'm writing these things because the teacher has told me to. It's bullshit." One day in sheer disgust, I figured, "I can write my own station," and I did it. I made up my own station. I just added the usual ingredients and "See, there is a station. I can come up with one too."

I went through writing the whole damn thing twice. I didn't feel a damn thing, so I gave up on it. What shifted it was that I started to get jealous, because I wanted all the Jedi powers that all the other people seemed to be developing. The assistants had amazing Jedi powers. They could see and feel things that I couldn't. I said, "How do you do it?" They said, "It's from writing the stations." So, I did it again.

The third time through, I started actually feeling it work. I started feeling freedom in Al-Itlaq, and in Al-Mahabba, I felt the love. I thought, "Okay, this makes absolutely no sense at all, given anything I know about words, writing, sentences or anything. Based on everything I have ever assumed about communication through language, this makes absolutely no sense. But clearly something is going on that has nothing to do with what I usually think of books as being for."

I also didn't like being told to cover my head. Why do I have to cover my head? What is this all about? I had plenty of objections to that.

People have different relationships to "should." My relationship to "should" is: fight like hell and do whatever the hell you want. Other people's relationship to "should" is more submissive, or a mixture of submit and fight at the same time. I always find it regrettable when people who are new to the path submit and fight simultaneously. They resist but don't actually come out with the resistance openly and honestly. I understand that this comes from the fear that if they object or resist, worse things will happen. They fear that they will be shunned and the door will close in some way.

I'm very glad that I experimented with fighting like hell against "should." It allowed me to find out that although the teachers really were inarguable about certain things, they didn't close their hearts to me when I argued with them. Sometimes they got a bit tired of it, but that's different from closing down. Meanwhile, I had my opportunity to not cover my head, to think that it was just a pile of nonsense and not have bad penalties for that. As a teaching assistant, I now really encourage students who don't want to do something to experiment with it. What happens when you do it, what happens when you don't do it? I tell them to be a scientist about it.

There came a time when I actually wanted to cover my head. It was in the middle of an airport. I was flying home from time at Sufi University, and it was clear that to preserve the state that I had gained at the university (which I very much wished to preserve) covering my head would feel really good. It was, in fact, very helpful. It created a kind of seclusion that allowed me to keep my state and be protected. I thought, "Huh, I'm glad that my teachers were not big obnoxious jerks about this like I was, so that I could change my mind without any big fuss being made about it. They allowed me to just go ahead and start wearing something on my head, if I wanted to. Not a problem".

There were a million things that I initially objected to. Sometimes there still are—and it's important to me to know that it will not be seen as bad or wrong for me to question and explore anything that doesn't feel right to me. I haven't been struck by lightning.

To remain at this inquiry, even if it's a form of disagreement, clearly is accepted in the tariqa community and by Sidi. That felt like a really important thing for me to know.

I've come a long way from fighting every inch of the way, to not having to agree with everything in a holy way and with an open heart and an open mind, waiting for deeper layers of understanding to come through.

## Maryam Thea Elijah, M.Ac.

Maryam Thea Elijah, L.Ac., has been a student of Chinese herbal medicine and acupuncture for over 30 years. She is the former director of the Chinese Herbal Studies Program at TAI Sophia Institute and the Chinese Herbal Studies Program at the Academy for Five Element Acupuncture.

She has apprenticed and studied with some of the most influential Chinese medicine teachers in the West. Maryam Thea is also a Muqaddam Teacher of the Shadhiliyya Sufi Order, and a teaching assistant at The University of Spiritual Healing and Sufism.

Maryam Thea maintains a private healing practice, that incorporates her Chinese medical knowledge and heart-centered healing. At the request of her clients and students, she has developed a series of workshops teaching Whole Heart Connection (formerly Medicine Without Form). They open the student to "healing" situations outside of formal health care contexts, including family life, classrooms, activism for social change, and work within organizational structures. She currently teaches Chinese Medicine, Sufi Healing, and Whole Heart Connection across the United States. Maryam Thea is based in Southern Vermont, where she lives with her family.

# How to be with Evil and Injustice

## Nafisa Janet Smith, M.Ac.

**Where the hell are you God? It's me, Nafisa. Do you even exist?**

One Sunday morning, many years ago, I accosted my minister and mentor at the time, complaining that I had already heard the sermon he had just preached. After listening to the umpteenth recycled sermon on the true nature of power, I was bored. My minister responded, "You're right. I've found that most of us have two or three themes which we keep coming back to over the course of our lives." "Interesting," I thought. "I wonder what my themes are?"

During that same period of my life, I read the book, *An Interrupted Life, the Diaries, 1941–43 and Letters from Westerbork* by Etty Hillesum. Etty Hillesum was a Dutch Jew who perished during the Holocaust. These were her diaries and letters from the end of her life. I was inspired and amazed at her zeal for life, her compassion and her faith that remained strong in the face of horrific evil.

Having struggled with depression most of my life, I longed for that same faith in humanity and a faith in something that transcended the daily life I knew.

I also met my husband during this time. Ivan was a refugee from the civil war in his native country El Salvador. During one of our first conversations, I gave him the book *Gandhi on Non Violence* to which he responded, "This is the theme of my life." For most of his life, he had struggled with the injustice he witnessed in El Salvador and the question of when and if violence was necessary to remedy these injustices.

After over twenty years together, my husband and I moved to El Salvador in 2012 to live in the house that his parents had built 50 years earlier. While the Salvadoran civil war ended in 1992, the violence never stopped and the economic disparities which led to the war were never resolved. In 2015, El Salvador had the highest homicide rate in the world, outside of an active war zone. While homicides decreased in 2016, the rate remains the highest of any country in the Western Hemisphere. Street gangs, widespread corruption, and money laundering for narco traffickers mar the beauty of this beautiful country, whose people are looking for hope and opportunity despite the difficulties many face.

A little over a year after moving to El Salvador, the 13-year-old daughter of our housekeeper disappeared. Our house borders a ghetto and the neighborhood in which we live is controlled by the street gang MS13. Many children in the neighborhoods surrounding where we live join the gangs, even though membership guarantees either an early death or imprisonment in some of the worst jails in the Western Hemisphere. The jails here often lack potable water, are horribly overcrowded (maybe 80 prisoners in a 12' x 14' cell) and the food, if provided at all, is barely edible.

Into the gang-controlled ghettos of El Salvador, Selena was born and eventually, like many children, she got caught up with the gangs. At the age of thirteen, she made a fatal mistake. She got involved with a leader in the rival gang—the 18th Street Gang. This is not permissible in an MS13 neighborhood. Once she had been exposed, she had no choice but to flee the country immediately, not telling her mother or other family what had happened. Where did she go? The rumor was that she went to Guatemala. Maybe she tried to get to the U.S. Most likely, she ended up prostituting her body somewhere and is now dead.

A week after Selena's disappearance, I travelled to the U.S. and saw one our teachers in the Sufi order of which I am a member. At that time, we still did not know what had happened. We only knew that for no apparent reason a young girl had disappeared. As I sobbed out my horror over Selena's disappearance, this teacher spoke to me about bowing to all of God's creation, even that which appears evil.

What the .....? It was easy to council but extremely difficult to comprehend. To me this was a zen koan—a riddle that made absolutely no sense to the mind. However, if only the heart could understand, maybe I could find some peace.

This was one of the themes in my life: How do I live in an unjust world in which violence is an everyday reality? How can I believe in a God that allows such horrible things to happen? Where was the compassion and the mercy? How was I to "be" with evil?

*To see a World in a Grain of Sand*
*and a Heaven in a Wild Flower*
*Hold Infinity in the palm of your hand*
*And Eternity in an hour.*

—William Blake from *Auguries of Innocence*

*Neither My heavens nor My earth can contain Me.*
*Only the heart of My faithful slave contains Me.*

—Hadith Qudsi

If we want to know the sweetness of honey, we must first taste it. Telling us that honey is sweet cannot convince us, if we do not personally taste its sweetness. The same is true with love. No one telling us that we contain the beauty and love of the universe in our innermost beings can convince us of this until we personally taste this love.

Looking outward at all the pain and destruction in the world only tore me apart and left me deeply despairing. To understand what it meant to bow to all of creation and to understand the statement that each human could contain something transcendent, I had to begin looking at the world and my place in this world in a fundamentally different way.

This necessitates a journey inward. Like many, when I turned my gaze inward, what I found seemed very far away from any sort of beauty or love. I found depression. I found anxiety. I found self-doubt and fear.

I have spent much of my life going between the two states of anxiety and depression. During one period in which the anxiety and depression was severe, I went to my shaykh, Sidi Muhammad al-Jamal and asked him what to do. The anxiety was bad. The depression was actually a welcome relief from the anxiety. And neither state left me wanting to live. Sidi responded:

*"Your husband loves you."*
*"I know Sidi, but what am I to do about this anxiety?"*
*"Your husband loves you very much."*
*"Yes yes, Sidi, but that's not my question."*
*"Your husband loves you very much."*

After the third time that Sidi responded, I realized that the answer to my question had something to do with learning how to receive love. I spent much of my life feeling disconnected from others. The internal voices that blocked a deeper connection to others did not make rational sense. However, they were there anyway, subtly controlling my life. Shame. Feelings of not being good enough. A strange hidden voice from childhood that whispered, "If you do something you are not supposed to and call attention to yourself, you will be killed." "Hide, it is safer." "Don't trust anyone. They will betray you."

All of these voices and many others were lurking in my subconscious. They were clouding my perception and creating a barrier to feeling any joy or love. Life events often validated the voices. I was betrayed. I did find myself in dangerous situations. I had many reasons to be ashamed of my life.

The Sufi tradition teaches us that our outer reality often mirrors our inner voices. Challenges in our outer lives thus become the grist for cleaning the inner voices that block our perceptions of a deeper transcendent reality.

When, for example, I find myself betrayed by another, instead of allowing that betrayal to validate the voice that I cannot trust anyone, I must go deeper, past the pain of betrayal and ask what voices are struggling to come out of the darkness and into the light to be cleaned? If my partner tells me he cannot trust me, is there are part of me that is not trusting him? Is there a part of me that is not trusting God? What is the outer reflecting to me of the inner?

In time, more and more voices can flush up from the subconscious, and as they come out in the open, we can clean them. How do we do this? We must first acknowledge that they exist. They are there, present for us, shaping our perception of reality. We then ask whatever higher power or higher wisdom we can believe in to help us go deeper. For those of us who have had a difficult time believing in anything transcendent, this requires a leap of faith.

That leap of faith was difficult for me, so I begin by focusing on my chest and repeating "hallelujah" which was as close as I was willing to come to the Arabic word for God, Allah. The "a" sound helps to open the chest and the "L" sound helps us to sink into the chest. In this way, I learned to connect with something deeper in my heart, so I could look with more objectivity at the voices circling in my head.

In time, hallelujah was replaced with Allah. As I delved more deeply into the Sufi path, I learned how useful chanting was in creating a vibration that helped dissolve voices that reverberated in my mind. These voices blocked me from knowing my own heart and discovering the love and the beauty that rested within.

*Tyger Tyger burning bright,*
*In the forests of the night;*
*What immortal hand or eye,*
*Could frame thy fearful symmetry?*

*In what distant deeps or skies*
*Burnt the fire of thine eyes?*
*On what wings dare he aspire?*
*What the hand, dare seize the fire?*

*And what shoulder, & what art,*
*Could twist the sinews of they heart?*
*And when thy heart began to beat,*
*What dread hand? & what dread fee?*

*What the hammer? what the chain,*
*In what furnace was they brain?*
*What the anvil? what dread grasp,*
*Dare its deadly terrors clasp!*

*When the stars threw down their spears*
*And water'd heaven with their tears:*
*Did he smile his work to see?*
*Did he who made the Lamb make thee?*

*Tyger Tyger burning bright,*
*In the forests of the night:*
*What immortal hand or eye,*
*Dare frame they fearful symmetry?*

—William Blake

On one of my earlier visits to El Salvador, prior to moving here, my husband and I visited El Mozote. From December 10–12, 1981, during the Salvadoran Civil War, the Atlacatl Battalion of the Salvadoran Army killed over 1000 civilians. Half of them were children who had taken refuge in the village after authorities had assured them that they would be safe. It was and remains the largest recorded massacre in the Western Hemisphere. Women and girls as young as 10 years of age were raped and tortured before being killed. There was only one survivor—a woman, Rufina Amaya, who somehow managed to hide in a tree after witnessing her husband's decapitation and hearing her children cry out for her, while they were being murdered. Her youngest child was only eight months old.

When Ivan and I were driving along the dirt road to El Mozote, I had a sense of foreboding, fearing what I might feel at a place where so much horror had taken place. Would I feel the ghosts of all those who had lost their lives? What was it like for the relatives who had returned and were rebuilding the village? Would they look at me, a wealthy gringa, with suspicion and hostility?

At the epicenter of where the massacre took place, on the side of the rebuilt Catholic church, there is a garden where the remains of many of the children are buried—El Jardine de Los Innocentes (Garden of the Innocents). With trepidation, I entered the garden. To my incredulous surprise, inside the garden I did not feel horror. I did not feel sadness. I was inundated by a sense of peace and love, and at that moment I knew in the core of my being, in some inexplicable illogical way, that despite the horrors these children had suffered, despite what their physical beings may have known and witnessed, their souls—that which had lived on after death—were at peace and surrounded by love.

Many converts to Islam struggle with the Qur'an, especially the passages in the Qur'an which speak of Allah's wrath and judgment. If Islam is about mercy, compassion and peace, what is all this fire and brimstone about?

For me, however, when I first read many of these passages dealing with "judgment day" and when I listened to the recitation of these passages in Arabic, I inexplicably felt joy. This did not make much rational sense. It has taken me a long time to understand why these passages give me joy, instead of the fear that many experience when reading them.

Each chapter of the Qur'an except one, begins with "In the name of the Merciful and the Compassionate." Therefore, we know from the beginning that the transcendent force referenced in the Qur'an is first and foremost, merciful and compassionate.

In order to stand strong in the face of the injustices and violence in the world, we must ground ourselves in this transcendent mercy and compassion. Without it, the horrors we read about, hear about and those we might experience ourselves are overwhelming.

I believe it was this transcendent mercy and compassion I felt many years ago when visiting El Jardin de los Innocentes in El Mozote. It was this mercy and compassion flooding through my being that allowed me to witness the atrocity that had happened without collapsing into fear.

It is only when we know at the core of our beings that there is something that transcends this world that we can have the faith to look, with eyes wide open, at what this world contains — both the good and the evil.

The passages of the Qur'an that speak of judgment, transport us to a different reality. It is a reality that is not limited to the physical world we live in. These passages open up the possibility that there is justice. It is a justice that we may not be able to see in this physical realm. However, it is an eternal justice and will come to pass. These passages open up the possibility that the souls of the innocent children of El Mozote may be at peace and resting in the light of love.

Allah says in His Qur'an that "They who are close to God, no fear shall they have nor shall they grieve." (10:62).

This is possible only when we have encountered another reality that transcends this world, which is based in the power of love and compassion.

To encounter this world, we must travel inward and taste for ourselves. The spiritual journey to God is a journey of clearing the veils and misperceptions that prevent us from tasting this love.

In the Sufi path, I have tasted this love and found the faith I longed for in my twenties, when I read Etty Hillesum's diaries. I cannot give this faith to others. We each must find it within ourselves. My hope is to inspire others to continue searching and looking within, so they too can taste this beauty that transcends this world and find the faith needed to bow to all of God's creation, that which we love and that which horrifies us.

## Nafisa Janet Smith, M.Ac.

Nafisa Janet Smith graduated from Duke University with a B.A. in East Asian Studies.

She had a varied career in the nonprofit sector and also worked in finance.

Nafisa later returned to school to get her Masters in acupuncture. She then practiced acupuncture for 10 years in Washington DC. Her acupuncture work focused primarily with patients who were HIV positive as well as people suffering from mental health issues ranging from schizophrenia to anxiety and depression.

Nafisa completed her studies at The University of Spiritual Healing and Sufism in 2007 and has continued studying Sufism at USHS and with Fawzia al-Rawi. She currently serves as a teaching assistant at USHS, and administers the Healing Certification Program and Student Healing Clinic at USHS.

# Finding Peace, Living Peace, Building Peace

## John Abd al-Qadir Davies, LL.B., M.Litt, M.S., Ph.D.

In my career as a peace maker, one of the most profound and life-changing experiences was taking part in a transformation from dictatorship to democracy in Indonesia. It was the most extensive work I had undertaken so far in a majority Muslim country, from 1999 to 2001, just after a popular, non-violent uprising had forced the end of a 30-year dictatorship under General Suharto. I worked with a small team to help those working toward a democratic transition in an archipelago of more than 13,000 islands, with over 200 million people speaking several hundred different languages. The country, which has an enormous diversity of ethnic, spiritual and cultural traditions, and exquisite natural beauty and biodiversity, is the largest majority Muslim country in the world, and awoke for me a deep interest in Islam.

Conflicts were breaking out, especially in places where native populations in the outer islands were finding themselves increasingly dominated by "transmigrants" from the more densely populated central islands of Java and Madura. With central government support, including cash and land grants, and better connections with the central government, they were often out-competing the local people, and were seen as undermining their local traditions. From Aceh and Kalimantan to Bali, Sulawesi, Maluku and Papua, we found local people resisting central rule from Java, not trusting the idea of a democracy where they would be permanently outnumbered and their identity threatened with subjugation or extinction.

In rural West Kalimantan, for example, I was introduced by a local NGO to leaders of the native Dayak people, who had recently seized the opportunity of the fall of the Suharto regime to ally with the Melayu to attack and ethnically cleanse the area of the Madurese transmigrants, now corralled into huge camps for the displaced. The Dayak told me how their traditions of collective use and care for the land and forests without private ownership were being displaced by the Madurese who came with government grants, fencing off "their" land, felling virgin forests to develop lucrative logging industries and often burning the remaining growth to establish massive palm-oil plantations. This contributed to an equally massive smog that regularly shut down shipping and airports across the region. The Dayak are mainly Christian, but had chosen to revive an old shamanistic tradition of head-hunting to create fear in the Madurese. They showed me some of the tools of the trade, including shrunken heads for display on poles, which apparently had had the desired effect.

They brought me to an isolated jungle retreat to mediate initially between them and the Melayu, a local Malay Muslim people who had joined them to defeat and evict the Madurese. The methods of the Dayak had clearly impacted the Melayu, whose trust for their neighbors and allies had been shaken by witnessing the brutal side of the Dayak tradition. The Dayak insisted on wearing their traditional dress (which included carrying a machete-like "sword" or knife) for the meeting. However, the Melayu were saying no way—leave your weapons at home. Our first challenge was how to honor the human needs of both sides—respect for tradition and identity on the one hand, safety on the other? We learned that the Dayak would sometimes wear miniature knives that were a few inches long, and both parties were persuaded to accept that concession, which opened the way for honest and respectful engagement. Each side listened to learn from the other, to understand their feelings and needs around the issues, and to lay the groundwork for consensus on how to sustain a partnership in addressing them. These issues ranged from redressing the mistrust between them, to pressuring the central government both to relocate the displaced Madurese to different islands and to stop all incoming transmigration, to protecting the forests and traditional ways of allocating and caring for the land, to working for greater autonomy from central government rule.

It was this strategy of working on the ground to contain or resolve local conflicts, networking with others to reach across the country, and building local capacity for peace as broadly as possible, that was critical in bringing the country through this chaotic period. People had to experience what working together (even with those you have fought against), using inclusive, democratic means looks like, before they could trust the idea of democracy for the country. Integrating indigenous methods, including what the Muslims called *"shura"* (making consensus decisions through consultation among stakeholders) and *"sulha"* (community reconciliation), and adapting them to restore their effectiveness where they were breaking down, ensured a sense of ownership of democratic traditions. The Ministers we worked with in Jakarta came to understand how important it was to delegate substantial governmental responsibilities to islands and regions with their own traditions, as part of a federal system that has allowed Indonesia to progress and provide inspiration to others in South-East Asia and the Islamic world.

After the two years of working in Indonesia followed by the devastating attacks on our own country on September 11, 2001, I focused my work for peace (as Co-Director of the Partners in Peacebuilding Program in the University of Maryland's Center for International Development and Conflict Management) increasingly in Muslim countries and countries with restive Muslim minorities, including Egypt, Israel/Palestine, Senegal, Pakistan, India, the Philippines, Azerbaijan and Turkey. Several of my partners and students in Egypt and Tunisia were active in the non-violent Arab Spring movement, succeeding in bringing transitions to democracy, though sadly losing ground again in Egypt, given the polarization between Islamist ideologues and the military. However, peace building is typically a long-term proposition requiring much patience (*sabr*).

Work on addressing internal, societal conflicts cannot be left exclusively to governments. They are too easily tempted to dismiss even non-violent challengers within the country as criminals, terrorists or worse. They cry that they have no-one they can negotiate with, seeking rather to suppress them even to force them off their land or out of the country, often setting the conditions for escalation or protraction of violence. Or they may be just afraid of the political risks of shifting from repression or confrontation to collaboration with the "enemy." So I have focused on peace building through "multi-track" diplomacy, seeking to bring together unofficial opinion leaders on opposing sides of a conflict, to map out viable pathways to peace that address the human needs of both/all parties. We help them to then engage official leaders on both sides, to help them see the possibilities and broad support for peace making, while also building the skills needed to sustain the work locally as well as nationally.[1] Almost 85% of those killed in the fighting in these societal wars, are non-combatant civilians (including as many women and children as men). Therefore, it is necessary to engage and mobilize civilians to open the way to peace, as happened in Indonesia, Tunisia, and briefly, Egypt, rather than leaving them to be recruited for, or victimized by, violence.

The most powerful model for my work, whom I met and took hand with in 2003, has been Shaykh Muhammad Sa'id al-Jamal ar-Rifa'i ("Sidi" to his students), a senior teacher (*imam*) at the al-Aqsa Mosque on the Haram al-Sharif/Temple Mount in Jerusalem, one of the most holy places in Islam as well as Judaism, with some of the holiest sites in Christianity close by. The site which, throughout his more than 40 years of tenure there, was at constant risk of violence following the Israeli takeover in 1967. When in 1968, a pro-Israeli radical set fire to the mosque, Sidi alerted, organized and led local Palestinians to fight and eventually contain the fire using buckets to carry water (they found the water mains to the Haram had been cut off by the municipality). He eventually prayed in the center of the blaze, before it could

---

1        John Davies and Edward Kaufman *Second Track/Citizens' Diplomacy: Concepts and Techniques for Conflict Transformation*. Lanham, MD: Rowman and Littlefield, 2003.

put the ancient building, first built 1300 years before, beyond repair. It was four hours before local, Jerusalem-based Israeli fire trucks arrived to finish the job with fire hoses, with Sidi taking a hose up to an opening in the roof to douse the flames in the wooden-beamed dome. On several occasions he confronted Israeli troops entering Al-Aqsa in search of terrorists, asking them to respect the holiness of the site, even to the extent of standing his ground in the face of a hail of bullets, some ripping through his jalaba but leaving him untouched, to the consternation of the soldiers.[2]

For decades, he worked to maintain peace and contain outbreaks of violence in the Holy Land in the face of oppression and periods of terrorist violence, inspiring many to the Sufi way of love. He opened a children's school in East Jerusalem, for example, that welcomed kids without regard to their religious affiliation. He found ways to admit the poorest who had nowhere else to go and no money to pay. He also ministered in diverse ways to the poor, the sick and others most in need throughout the Land. He was guided to come to the US each summer and fall beginning in 2000, working to plant the seeds of real peace in this country, knowing how critical that was for the whole world. Given the unfortunate evolution of events both in Jerusalem and the US since his passing in late 2015, it is hard to miss the truth of his words, and the need for us to do all we can to take up his work.

Later he explained to me that I could do more for the Holy Land, and the other countries I was working with, through working for peace in the US (given its outsized impact on support for peace or war around the world) than I could accomplish through my visits to work directly for peace in the region. "Make peace in your own country," he said, by "working to fly the flag of peace in every home." This echoed for me the multi-track strategy of building peace from the grass roots up, and I feel blessed to have been able to take his advice and focus my work here, working through both the University of Spiritual Healing and Sufism and the University of Maryland, as well as with

---

2       Sidi Shaykh Muhammad Sa'id al-Jamal ar-Rifa'i *The Guide: Teachings, Stories and Descriptions of the Life of Shaykh Muhammad Sa'id al-Jamal ar-Rifa'i*. Sidi Muhammad Press, 2014.

individuals, couples, families and communities through the Farm of Peace.

Sidi worked with me particularly to clarify the practice of *sulha* (reconciliation) as it was practiced by the Prophet Muhammad (peace and blessings upon him). Given the poor understanding of *sulha* in contemporary Muslim cultures, and the gross distortion of Islamic teachings on peace by militant "Islamist" ideologues, this is a critical element for restoring peace in the Arab region and in the world, which I have continued to use to good effect with non-Muslim as well as Muslim students, couples, families and communities in the US, some of whom have taken it back to their country of origin.

More fundamentally, the Sufi teachings and practices emphasize the inner work required to find peace in our own hearts, healing the wounds that can otherwise pull us into separation—seeing ourselves as individuals under threat in a hostile world. When I asked Sidi where the teachings on peace are in his books, he told me they were everywhere, but especially in the teachings about love. It was this search for a spiritual path based on opening the heart to love that had led me to Sidi in the first place, and his teaching of a profound form of Sufism I had not yet encountered. When Jamila and I finally met him, without any introduction, he read my heart as if he had long known all about my search, welcomed us and held us in a deep love that answered all my questions. He embodies his teaching that love is the key to bridging the apparent gap between us, or between us and Allah. Sufi practices, such as *dhikr* (remembrance) of Allah, in which we open our heart to align or resonate with the Divine Heart, and *tawba* (turning our heart to Allah to ask His forgiveness for however we may have harmed others or ourselves), open our awareness to Divine presence and acceptance of His love, compassion, guidance, healing and peace. Love deepens as we come to know Him more deeply, and to recognize Him in the heart of those He puts in front of us, until it finds its culmination in unity, where we experience our souls, our higher selves, as no longer separate from Him or from His creation, but as expressions of the one Divine soul.

The core of peacemaking is grounding ourselves in this unity where there is no "other," being the peace, before presuming to help others find it. "Doctor, heal thyself" applies as much to peacemaking as to healing. Once, for example, when I was about to greet Sidi before teaching a USHS class on peacemaking, he called out sternly to me, "I will pray for you!" He had read my heart and saw that I was grumbling to myself about someone I had some difficulty with, so I thanked him and went off to make *tawba* and teach the class from a different place. When I saw him next morning my heart was clear and at peace again, and this time he was beaming and inviting me to come sit with him.

This principle of being the peace was brought home to me even more clearly when my wife Jamila had been suffering from *grand mal* seizures for several years. They were becoming stronger and more frequent, and the doctors she asked for help could do nothing to stop it. Her daughter had eventually died of the condition at age 10, so we were both deeply concerned. We had asked Sidi about it years before, when the seizures were still partial, but I couldn't understand what he was saying when he turned and spoke severely to me. Then one night when I awoke to find her thrashing wildly around in the bed, the usual precursor to a full seizure, it suddenly dawned on me that I had still been thinking of her as a separate person with a disease I had to help her to heal, rather than as a reflection or face of myself, and my need to heal and release the stress I was carrying. I immediately made *tawba* for my mistake in seeing her as other. Being a profoundly sensitive and empathic woman, seizures were a (brutal) way for her to release that stress for both of us. The moment I dropped from there into a state of surrender into the unity of Allah (*dhikr* of the heart), the thrashing stopped. It was the first time ever that it stopped without a full seizure. Her face was perfectly at peace, relaxed, radiant as she lay, still completely asleep. Later, I remembered when Sidi had spoken severely to me in response to our question about the early seizures, and realized he was pointing to the stress I put myself under in my work and travels in unstable or violent situations, was impacting her even more. When I told him about the healing, he beamed his approval. A couple of months later, the same thing happened, exactly, with the seizure stopping the instant I made tawba—and after that there were no more episodes. It's been several years since, and I am filled with gratitude for the deepening gifts of love that have followed.

*Tawba* and *dhikr* are at the core of the *sulha* process, which I have used to reconcile and bring peace to many communities in several countries and to reconcile divided nations. We adapt the method to harmonize with local traditions, to return them to effectiveness in a way that allows local people to accept ownership and responsibility for continuing to apply them.[3]

*Dhikr* shares some fundamental characteristics with the forms of deep meditation that I had practiced and researched for years before taking hand with Sidi. I shared with Sidi some of the results, including reduced stress, improved health and longevity[4] and the revolutionary finding that large groups practicing together intensify exponentially the profound field effects of meditative practices in reducing societal violence and facilitating efforts for peace. For example, over a series of seven group meditation initiatives (involving between 100 and 7,000 people, including Muslims, and lasting 1–12 weeks each), both within and at varying distances from the Lebanon war in the early 80's, we found an average reduction of over 75% in war deaths in Lebanon during and immediately after each group initiative.[5] An eighth group of 10,000 in 1987–88 set the conditions for a final peace agreement (the Taif Accords) in 1989. Sidi accepted the results, saying "Yes, this is what happens in our *khalwas*" (extended group practice of silent *dhikr*), and this has been my experience as well.

---

3    John Davies, Wubalem Fekade, 'Mamphekeleli Hoohlo, Edward Kaufman and 'Mamochaki Shale "Partners in Peacebuilding in Lesotho." In Craig Zelizer and Robert Rubinstein (eds.) *Building Peace: Practical Reflections from the Field*. Kumarian Press, 2009.
4    Charles Alexander, Ellen Langer, John Davies et al. "Meditation, Mindfulness and Longevity: An Experimental Study with the Elderly," *Journal of Personality and Social Psychology,* 57 (6), 950-964, 1989.
5    John Davies and Charles Alexander "Alleviating Political Violence: Impact Assessment Analyses of the Lebanon War." *Journal of Social Behavior and Personality,* 285-338, 2005.

After Sidi's passing, and with the continuing, divisive impact of the recent federal elections and new policies discriminating against Muslim and Hispanic immigrants and refugees, curtailing women's rights and dignity, reducing access to health care for the poor, rejecting the various UN decisions protecting Palestinian rights, and the Paris Accords so central to stopping the acceleration of climate change, it has become clear that it is necessary for us as Sufis, to not only come together to deepen our own inner and outer work for peace, but also to play our part in building a broad coalition or network for peace in this country and beyond, including especially all those groups among us who are most at risk (African Americans and Jews are still far more likely than Muslims to be victims of hate crimes, for example, and women and Latino immigrants are still more widely discriminated against). We need to learn more deeply how to follow the Prophetic example and Qur'anic teachings of avoiding aggression, while speaking truth to power with a heart at peace, helping to restore justice for those who have been harmed, praying for Allah's mercy, guided by love, relying on our deepening connection with Allah.

I was able join with other Sufis in the Women's March on Washington just a few weeks before this writing, the day after the presidential inauguration. Close to three million people in the US, including half a million in Washington DC alone, and others in nearly 700 cities around the world, created a level of inspiration and excitement I haven't felt in a mass gathering before. There was no violence or arrests. People of all colors, genders and creeds gathered together, speaking, dancing, praying, chanting and cheering for social justice for women, blacks, immigrants, Muslims, refugees, LGBTQ, the environment, workers not able to earn a living wage, and the disabled. They carried signs that were overwhelmingly inclusive ("Pro-All-of-Life," "Make America Kind Again," "Black Lives Matter," "Equal Rights, Equal Pay," "We the People are Greater than Fear"). There were even some police among the thousands wearing pink hats to honor women's dignity and rights, others wearing pink statue-of-liberty headgear to welcome refugees and migrants, or Muslim Americans wearing American-flag-themed hijabs.

Echoes of this gathering continue in response to regressive policy measures such as blocking Muslims from seven countries from entering the country, or pulling out of the Paris climate accords, with several foreign countries and American states and cities, religious groups and non-government organizations moving to compensate by directly helping those immigrants impacted to protect their human rights, and several American states and cities (including potentially all 128 US cities that have joined the Global Covenant of Mayors) committing to uphold our obligations for limiting our excessive contributions to climate change.

What is Allah asking of us in these "interesting times" of polarization over not just policy, but the values that our nation stands for and we stand for? This includes values such as justice, compassion, peace and freedom; dignity, truth, kindness, caring, respect, strength, humility and love – loving for our brothers and sisters what we love for ourselves. Allah stretches us through adversity, so we can discover what we are capable of. We can realize and sustain the values that represent the soul of the nation and the soul of the human race, both through deepening the inner work that is needed to truly embody these divine values that represent our higher, God-given human nature, and also through accepting responsibility (as *khalifa*) for putting our unique gifts into constructive action to help and protect others in need, whatever their race, religion, gender or beliefs.

# John Abd al-Qadir Davies, LL.B., M.Litt, M.S., Ph.D.

   John Abd al-Qadir Davies is Visiting Associate Professor and Co-Director of Partners in Peacebuilding at the University of Maryland's Center for International Development and Conflict Management, co-founder of the Masters in Peacemaking Program at the University of Spiritual Healing and Sufism and Director of the Living Peace Program at the Farm of Peace.

   After practicing law and psychology and teaching meditation in Australia, he moved to the US in 1982. He has trained thousands of professionals in conflict transformation, prevention and multi-track diplomacy, including political leaders and diplomats, UN peacekeepers, police, educators, religious, traditional and civil society leaders. He has led peace initiatives in over 30 countries around the world, co-developed conflict and genocide early warning systems for the US government and international coalitions and trained UN peace keepers from many countries. He served as a consultant to various

US departments and international governments and organizations. He has conducted extensive research on the impact of spiritual and secular techniques in promoting peace, which has been published widely.

He mediates conflicts between couples and within communities, organizations and families and leads retreats and workshops for those seeking peace and reconciliation at all levels of life.

# Four Lessons I Learned about the Truth of the Feminine

## Mastura Debra Graugnard, M.Div.

How does a young girl learn what it means to be a woman? Unfortunately, too much of the role modeling comes from the media, which depends on news that sensationalizes and shocks in order to sell.

When I was young, media was television and print magazines. They sent a strong consistent message that the tall, slender, scantily clad, seductive women were the ones who commanded attention and admiration. These women turned heads, stopped men in their tracks and left them with their tongues hanging out.

There's a lot of power in that! It's much more gratifying than the oppressing messages that tell us what women can't do. "Women are not good at math and science." "A woman needs to stay home and have dinner on the table when her husband gets home from work." "The woman is the weaker partner in the relationship."

However, the resultant lure has not been healthy for women or men. Neither pole honors the truth of either gender. The polarities contribute to issues such as food addiction and eating disorders, promiscuity, sexual assault, shaming and even suicide.

Unfortunately, the whole mix of messages still permeate our culture. We need to heal from the false impressions that have been burned into the psyche of so many women and men over many decades.

Healing means wholeness. It brings honor and respect for all parts of ourselves, inner and outer. It brings about balance and harmony on an individual and collective scale.

This begins with every woman, young and mature, knowing the truth of the feminine which is rarely told.

I chose to tell this story with the hope that every young girl and woman know the truth of how sacred she is, and embody the self-respect and inner strength that comes with that knowing.


In younger years, I was the most insecure person I've known, craving attention, begging for friendship. I'd do just about anything to get people to like me.

At about two weeks old, I had experienced heart failure. I don't know much about it because my mother would never talk about it. However, I had a marker on my life that kept it at the forefront of my consciousness.

I grew up with black teeth. They were stained from medication I was given in the hospital. My teeth were like little charcoals in my mouth.

Everywhere I went, I tried not to open my mouth. However, eventually I would. I had a childhood friend who would threaten me when we would go places together: "Whatever you do, don't you dare open your mouth!" But I couldn't help it. A smile or a laugh – something would expose my pearly blacks.

It always got the same response. "Ooh, gross! What happened to your teeth? What's wrong with your mouth?"

Wherever there were kids around, the honest creatures that they are, I drew a crowd. Not for the reasons I wanted. I wanted to be liked and accepted. Instead, I was abhorred and rejected.

I would just stoically stand there and in a single breath recite the phrase I had been taught before I could remember. "When I was a little baby, I had heart failure, and I had to take medicine that made my teeth turn black."

Then at four years of age, the ugly girl with black teeth got some attention. I was molested by a teenage boy. You might know the feeling – unfortunately, all too many women do, and men, too. Now you've got a secret, a profound secret. You know that it was wrong and you're left with shame, trying to hide something even though no one would be able to tell unless you told them – or unless you somehow became different.

I know now that girls and boys do become different, even from one experience and even if they don't tell. At least that was my experience. It changes something in you. There is a mix of knowing, keeping a secret, hiding something, fear and shame, yet discovering something new and being unsure of what to do with it.

I was molested again at 9, and again at 12. Though I had fought and resisted at the time, after the age-12 incident, I decided I might as well go for it.

I was beginning to understand the power of the feminine. The kid who had felt abhorred and rejected had learned the secret to getting all the attention and respect I wanted.

So I did.

It was the dawn of the sexual revolution. I was discovering what it meant to become a woman by watching television. Southwest airlines commercials turned heads with the sex goddesses of the sky. "I'm Debbie, come fly me!" Cher was knocking everybody out with her outfits on the Sonny and Cher show. These became role models.

Binge drinking, drugs, sex and rock and roll. I could be everything society told me to be and all that men wanted me to be. I became obsessed with becoming as popular as I could in the only way I knew how.

Fast forward to around age 30, when I had a lightning bolt spiritual awakening. I suddenly saw life through new eyes, with a realization of what love is. I knew things had to change. I was changed on the inside, so I had no choice.

At the time, I had a boyfriend and had stopped using drugs. I held a corporate job and was taking care of myself. Yet, in an uncomfortable situation, such as walking into a room of new people who were obviously going to be disgusted by me, I would binge drink and often black out.

However, with the spiritual epiphany, these ways of coping and earning acceptance didn't work anymore. I saw the truth about what I had been doing. A light was shined on the shadow, and I couldn't do that anymore.

So I started seeking help. I first found a charismatic Christian church that I really liked. It opened me up in many ways. It connected me with others who had been through similar experiences. I began my healing journey there.

Soon, I moved about an hour away. I again found a charismatic Christian church that welcomed me in. Shortly after I joined, the pastor announced they were having a friends and family day. We were to invite as many people as we could.

The next day at work, I set out on the mission of inviting everyone I knew. I was working in a high-tech firm that employed a diverse population from the US and many other countries.

The first person I talked to was my team leader. She said, "But I'm Jewish." I said, "Oh? What does that mean?" Her explanation softened my heart.

The next person I talked to was Baha'i, then Hindu and then Muslim. With each inquiry, I learned more about the beliefs, morals and values of the other faiths. What was most striking for me was how each one incorporated practices into their daily lives that honored their beliefs.

This was what I wanted! I wanted to know how to LIVE my faith, not just show up for a church experience on Sundays. The conditioning from my childhood ran so deep in me, that even though my heart had been changed and I had awakened to a love that was real, I still didn't know how to be and what to do in social situations. I was still living old patterns. It was as if I could watch myself and my behaviors from outside. I wanted desperately to LIVE my faith, but I didn't know how.

I later stopped by the church to talk to the pastor about what I had learned. Unfortunately, he told me that regardless of how devout my co-workers were in their faiths, if they didn't take Jesus Christ as their savior, they would go to hell.

Since then, I've met many Christians along my journey who are very loving, accepting and honoring of people of other faiths. However, this was a part of the lesson I needed to learn at that stage of my journey.

I could not accept that pastor's answer. I left that church knowing I would never return. I went home and found myself on my knees sincerely praying from a deep sincere place in my heart.

The words that were coming from my heart that night were a surprise to me. I was praying for a teacher or a guide to come and take me by the hand and show me how to live in a way that honored what I felt in my heart.

After that prayer, I stood up. "What did you just ask for? What were you doing on your knees?" I had been pretty sheltered as far as the spiritual world was concerned. I didn't know that things like spiritual teachers and guides even existed. How could I be asking for one?

However, almost instantly, the guide began to show up. For the first few years, the guide showed up only in spirit and began teaching me. I was learning about healing and how memories, beliefs and patterns got stored in the body. I learned about how forgiveness could lift whole sheets, like grids, that held beliefs and patterning in the tissues of the body. I learned about how unraveling situations could lead to an inner yearning for love, and these places were still waiting inside to receive the love they had wanted all along.

I learned that the existence of a powerful love, the love that had been shown to me in the awakening experience, had the power to heal anything –

physical, emotional, mental, energetic or spiritual! All of this made perfect logical sense to me, even though I had never heard of it before.

Soon, through divine guidance, I met my spiritual teacher in person. He was Sidi Shaykh Muhammad al-Jamal, a Sufi master from Jerusalem. I knew instantly when I saw him. I walked into the room at the Shadhiliyya Sufi Retreat Center in Pope Valley, California. He was sitting on the floor in the front of the room with several people gathered around.

When my eyes landed on him, the shell around my heart cracked open. My heart completely melted and spilled out onto the floor. He saw me and called me to come up to the front of the room. He asked me what was in my heart. I was afraid he had seen the bad stuff, so I decided to play dumb. "I don't know."

He said, "A deep, deep longing for God." Then he put his hands on my head and said some prayers in a language I didn't understand. I was filled with a high vibration, and my feet did not touch the ground for a week. It was another transformation experience beyond words, but as I recall the experience, I can feel my heart weep with gratitude.

Over the next eighteen years, Sidi made it his mission to get me to know my value as a human being and the significance of the value of a woman.

He had his work cut out for him. I was cloaked in many layers of confusion and mixed messages from family dynamics, childhood experiences and societal beliefs. Thank goodness, he didn't give up!

Not long after that meeting, I left the high-tech corporate world, gave away all my material possessions, sold my house and one car, then loaded up my truck and my pets and moved to California.

There I could live in spiritual community, immerse myself in the spiritual teachings and serve a mission of teaching what the world really needed to know in order to live in truth.

The first seven of those years were spent with no dating and no intimate connections with men—only discovering me. I never knew what it was like to just be with me, turning everything to face God, no matter what happened— whether by myself or in crowds. This was often intensely painful, but the best gift I could have received.

I experienced the depths of my loneliness and allowed my heart to break, only to be rebuilt and renewed. It was made whole again, and again and again.

There is a poem by the poet Hafiz:

*Don't surrender your loneliness so quickly.*
*Let it cut more deep.*
*Let it ferment and season you, as few human or divine ingredients can.*
*Something missing in my heart tonight has made my eyes so soft,*
*my voice so tender,*
*my need for God absolutely clear.*

I had surrendered my loneliness to God. The pain was gone. I didn't need to surrender my loneliness to anyone else ever again.

**Lesson #1: I didn't need anyone else's love to complete me. I was complete and whole in God alone.**

Of course, there was more to learn. I had learned to be secure and self-sufficient. It was now time for a relationship.

With no concern for finding a relationship, I decided to attend a spiritual gathering with my teacher at the Farm of Peace, a Sufi retreat center in Pennsylvania.

That's where it happened. I met someone. We had a lot in common –

love for animals, plants and nature, a passion for the health of the planet and fairness for all people. We talked for three days straight. Then we went to talk with Sidi.

Sidi confirmed all of the things that we had in common and offered to make the holy marriage between us right then and there. We insisted we needed time to discuss this. Going into the weekend, neither of us had expected such a significant event. Sidi said, "Sure. Take time. Take space."

We started off for a walk, then soon turned around and rushed back to Sidi. "With your permission and blessing, we would like to make the holy marriage."

It was 11 pm on a Saturday, under the full moon, covered by the awning of our friends' Airstream camper. We sat before Sidi. He joined our hands and blessed our union.

Afterwards, we turned around to see at least a hundred people watching. Some of them were cheering, while others were weeping. The sky had opened up and it was pouring rain on the crowd. This was supposedly a sign of good luck and a blessing on the marriage.

It took about six months to prepare to move. I then relocated to the East Coast to make a new life with my beloved.

Soon after I arrived, he, shall we say, freaked out. He couldn't believe what we had done without really knowing each other and without having dated. He was regretting his decision and strongly rejecting me. He said he wasn't attracted to me, he didn't love me and he didn't want to be with me.

Hmmm... What now? Well, of course, I understood he was just going through a phase. It was just issues from his past coming up to be healed. He would get through this and we'd live happily ever after. It was, after all, a holy marriage made by our spiritual teacher—meant to be until eternity, right?

I, therefore, decided to contain whatever he was going through with love and compassion, and just wait patiently. In the face of rejection, I could be stoic and wait for the moment to pass, just as I had done as a kid with black teeth.

At the one-year anniversary of our marriage, after six months of living together, our teacher returned for a gathering at the Farm of Peace. We went to see him, and this time, my beloved had a different question.

"Sidi, I don't love her. I'm not attracted to her. This was a mistake. I don't want to be with her. Will you please dissolve the marriage?"

Sidi looked at me and asked, "So what do you say about this?" I replied, "Oh Sidi, I understand he is just going through his resistance. I can wait for him." I thought I was being the holy and patient traveler—the good wife.

Then my beloved left the room. Sidi turned to me and said sternly, "Why you want to be with someone who not love you? He not polite with you! Not be weak. Be strong!"

He turned to his translator, Amany, and asked, "Where is my stick?" She handed him his cane. He drew a line in the dirt in front of him. He said, "You draw line in the sand. He cross this line, you hit him with stick! Not let someone treat you this way."

To be clear, my beloved had only been honest about his feelings. He had not done anything to harm me. However, I was given an opportunity to heal another pattern—staying in relationships that were not respectful, without speaking up for what I needed or commanding any respect for myself.

**Lesson #2: I must command respect for myself and not let someone into my heart unless they treat me with love and respect.**

I learned to expect to be respected, but there was another level to being a woman that I honestly had no idea existed.

A few years later, I went to Jerusalem for a trip hosted by Sidi's son, daughter-in-law and a long-time student.

Having grown up in the United States, my knowledge of other countries and cultures was shaped by the media. I had always heard that women in the Middle East were oppressed, disrespected and abused. I was actually a bit uneasy about the trip. Would this happen to me?

What I learned was a big surprise. During the trip, we were hosted by friends and students of Sidi's family. They were very gracious and loving. Each of them carried a genuine persona that was solid and certain. They lived to love and serve God. They treated us and each other with considerable respect and care. It was truly profound!

There was something about the relationships between the men and women that really caught my attention. I observed silently for days. Then at dinner on the last night of our trip, I had to ask. "The way you relate to each other as husband and wife is different from what I'm used to seeing in my country. Can you help me understand it?"

Sidi's son explained that his wife, as a woman, is created by God and made of God's love. She is worthy of love, honor and respect, and no less. She doesn't need to earn that. It's what God created. She doesn't need to deflect that, because it's not about her. It's about what God created.

He sees her and knows her as a holy being of God's creation. He treats her with love, because that's what she is. He honors and protects the space around her, as she walks in all her beauty and grace through the world.

He was putting words to what I had witnessed. I realized that if someone treated me that way, I might feel uncomfortable. However, it was pure beauty to witness.

I turned to her and asked, "How is this for you?" She looked at me almost puzzled. "Well, of course. This is the way it is." There was no arrogance or hierarchy. No lording over or subservience. Nor was she being placed on a pedestal from which she would certainly fall. There was no competition. They mutually cared for each other and respected each other.

The respect shown to the women I met during this trip, as well as the manner in which they received the respect, was new to me. It was a profound teaching. It gave me a glimpse of what God had made in me as a woman. The teaching continued as I returned home. I spent hours in meditation, calling to Sidi's spirit yet again to teach me the truth of this.

Through another of his daughters-in-law, I learned a lesson about the quality of God's compassion. Compassion is a bridge between the worlds. I could understand that compassion can move a judgmental heart into a loving state. When we find compassion for something or someone we are upset with, the compassion restores love and acceptance in our hearts for the situation or person. This moves us from the world of separation into the world of unity. That makes sense, and I had experienced it many times along the healing journey.

What I learned from Sidi's daughter-in-law, Fawzia, is that the name for the womb is from the same root as the word for compassion. The nature of the womb is compassion, and the womb of the woman is also a bridge between the worlds.

The Qur'an says that God sends compassion before us. His Compassion, ar-Rahman, precedes us in this life.

The woman's body is a bridge between the worlds and a bridge of God's compassion. A woman can bring life from the spirit realms into this material realm, by God's will. The nature of the womb of the woman is compassion. It is from love and it is a way to return to love. This is the sacred nature of the creation of the woman.

There is a Native American proverb that sums up this teaching:

*A woman's highest calling is to lead a man to his soul, so as to unite him with the Source.*

*A man's highest calling is to protect the woman so she can walk
the earth unharmed.*

**Lesson #3: The woman is created as a sacred being. Her divine essence is
a bridge between the worlds, a bridge to Source. She carries the wisdom
of earth and spirit. She is a nurturer and protector of life, a knower and
connector of the subtle realms, with true power beyond worldly physical
strength.**

With this newfound knowledge, I wanted every woman in the world
to know how sacred and beautiful she is. I want each woman to know with
complete certainty that she is worthy of love, honor and respect.

This is not something to be earned, and it cannot be destroyed. It is what
is because it is what God made.

So, how do we as women carry this truth in the world, even in the many
cultures that do not get how sacred we are?

This leads to the final lesson for this chapter.

Somewhere along the way, growing up, I acquired the image that God
was a man with a long white beard sitting on a throne above the clouds. Adam
was created in God's image, then he sacrificed a rib so that Eve could be
created and he could have a playmate.

Eve, in her weakness, then disobeyed God, listened to the devil and
doomed all of mankind to a life of suffering. So much for Adam's great
sacrifice. For the actions of the ungrateful slut, women must endure great pain
in labor, and all of mankind must suffer!

Though I learned a more merciful rendition of this story later in life, the
teachings of the early childhood years leave imprints on the psyche that have

to be cleaned energetically. The imprints are represented by those sheets and girds that get stored in the body that I mentioned early in the chapter.

The teaching of Adam and Eve in the Sufi tradition is much different from what I had grown up with. It goes like this:

> When God decided He wanted to create the world, He created Adam. When Adam was still in spirit form, God put His image in Adam, His light in him and the fragrance of all His qualities in Adam. God put the knowledge of everything from the seen and unseen, and the hidden and revealed, into the heart of Adam, and from Adam's breath, the universe was created. Adam, created in the image of God, contained the entire universe within him.
>
> In this state, Adam was turned completely to God and only wanted to be with God. In order to turn Adam to the created world to populate the world, God put the ego self into Adam. The ego self contains three parts — the desire to eat from the fruit and then to eliminate, the desire to sleep with the woman and make children and the desire to be king of the creation.
>
> God covered the light of His image in the human being with veils of darkness and light. The role of the keeper of the darkness, known in this language as Iblis, is to purify the veils so that the human would come to know himself or herself and reveal the truth of the original essence contained within, which is the image of God.
>
> Adam and Eve were separated into male and female in spirit form, and both contain the image of God, the light of God and all of His qualities. God has no form and no gender, yet the image of God is contained in all of creation.
>
> We are Adam, and we are Eve.[1]

The truth of God's essence is veiled and contained within every heart.

---

1      Sidi Shaykh Muhammad Sa'id al-Jamal ar-Rifa'i as-Shadhuli, *Music of the Soul*, Sidi Muhammad Press. 2002.

The task of each of us as sons and daughters of Adam and Eve is to preserve the secrets veiled inside the density of darkness and light of the material world, and to allow our veils to be purified by the fire in order to return us to the essence of our original nature.

The secrets we contain inside, the holiest of the holy, the sacred light, are to be protected and preserved within us. It is a sacred space and a union between each of us individually and God—our own personal intimate connection with Source.

When we come to know this with certainty in our bones and in our hearts, we can BE the strength, power, light and love of God in the world, and still protect the innermost sacred space in our bodies, hearts and souls, preserving it only for God. If we should allow another into our sacred space, it is only for the beloved who chooses to join us there as a worship and reverence of God's essence contained within us.

In this Sufi tradition, my teacher gives each of his students a name according to the nature of the essence they carry inside and the lessons they need to learn in life. My name is Mastura, which means hidden and protected. This is my lesson – to know, protect and preserve the light of God within me as I move through the world.

To some extent, we all share each other's lessons, since we are all mirrors for each other, reflecting for each other the light of God and informing each other of how we relate to the light of God we carry inside. We are here to help each other learn and grow, and to find our truth.


**Lesson #4: The sacred light we each carry inside is to be protected and preserved as an intimate space for our union with God.**


I am still in a physical body, and that's how I know the lessons are not complete. And there are more than what is listed here—this is only a Drop in the Ocean. However, as I look back on what I've received from these four main themes, all I can do is shake my head in awe.

Each of us carries the knowing of the divine essence. For some it is more veiled than others, but for every woman and every man, too, it is worthy of love, honor and respect.

If I could reach into the heart of every girl and woman in this world and flip that switch to turn on the light that illuminates her truth, I would.

I know this truth now. I have this truth now, and so do you!

## Mastura Debra Graugnard, M.Div.

Mastura Debra Graugnard has worked for The University of Spiritual Healing and Sufism since 1998. She is currently serving as University Relations Coordinator and teaching as guest faculty on topics related to healing your relationship with food and body image.

Mastura's journey began with the "incurable" diseases of hypoglycemia, fibrocystic disease and ulcerative colitis, which led her on a journey to find healing for the body, mind, heart and spirit.

She now helps people throughout the world to discover the health they want, the joy they deserve and the love that they are!

Mastura Debra is a spiritual healing practitioner, teacher and writer. She has been a student of Sufism for twenty years, and holds a Masters of Divinity in Spiritual Healing and Counseling. She established Joyfully Living Wellness, her private practice, and The Community for Conscious Living, an online community dedicated to healing the planet through Personal Transformation and Universal Harmony.

# Trauma and Grief: Pathways to Unlocking Trust

## Carol Maryam Reimer, M.S.T.

I remember pondering how one small incident in my childhood could have such a profound impact on my life more than 40 years later. One day, I was driving to town with one of my teachers and mentors, and I asked him that question. I expected a long explanation combining elements of spiritual healing and the gnosis of Sufism. Instead, his answer was simple. I am likely paraphrasing him, but his answer was a simple word: Trust. My ability to trust had been broken by a man who I never really knew. To this day, I still don't know his name.

As I sat down to write this chapter, I looked up the conventional definition of trust. According to dictionary.com, trust includes believing, expecting confidently, hope, to have confidence in, and implies a sense of safety.

I've often looked back at my life and my path to Sufism, with this question: "How did this broken trust play out and how did it bring me to where I am?" I want to clarify one thing. This reflection was not merely a mental exercise. It was an attempt to unravel unhealthy patterns and to advance the healing process. Before diving deeper into that self-reflection, let me tell you a little about my story and that childhood incident that made trust all but disappear in my life.

I grew up as the youngest of five children of a stay-at-home Mom and an engineer Dad. My middle sister contracted polio when she was just an infant. Needless to say, my Mom's hands were full most days. One day when I was about two, I decided that I wanted to go to the playground. Not the small one at the school at the end of the street, but the big one in the park on the other side of Loch Raven Blvd.—a four-lane, busy road. Not surprisingly, I wouldn't take no for an answer. What two-year-old does?

I can sort of still "hear" my thoughts from that long ago day. I'll do it myself! I set off to the playground to swing on the swings! What happened at the park is the script of parents' nightmares. I can't share many details with you because, by God's grace, I don't know them. Even all these years later, the details that I've come to know are limited and can be best shared through simple words: an older man, swings, the park, and me at age two. Even these limited details were buried for more than 40 years. Only the family tale of me going to the park on my own was remembered.

How does one get from buried memories to Sufism and learning to trust again? It was a journey through a lot of loss, grief, and heartache. When I was asked to contribute to this book, I've generally viewed the chapter's focus as connected to healing from childhood trauma. The real question is, how do you define childhood trauma?

My time spent as a writer and editor as well as a state and local tax consultant has exposed me not only to the power of words, but also to the wide-ranging meanings and interpretations. In my life, the definition of trauma expands beyond the swings and buried memories. I want to thank my friend for shining the light so that I could understand that all of it needs to be included, because each event represents a thread in the tapestry or a stepping stone on the journey. Choose your metaphor.

**Beyond the swings**

I was raised in a family that sincerely believed in God and His love and mercy. We went to church every Sunday. My parents, siblings, and I were always involved with whatever church we belonged to. Church and God were part of my daily life. I am very grateful for that. My family was filled with laughter, storytelling, and playing lots of games. My parents would get the family a new board game each Christmas. Oh, the wonderful memories! I even remember my brother Eric playing kick-the-can or my sister Judy playing kickball with my friends and me. My brother is 13 years older, and my sister is 7 years older. It was an extraordinary family.

My life was also full of loss and grief. I guess you could say it started when I was five with the loss of my paternal grandfather, and continued on with the loss of my sister and Dad about three years later. My maternal grandmother passed a few years later and a couple of uncles. I think that you get the picture. Yet, their spirits always remained part of our lives. We continued to tell those family stories that every family has. Remember the time that Dad turned off the electricity to the house before we left on vacation? That reminds me of when Joanie used to pull the hair on Eric's legs to pay him back. Remember when Joanie got stuck in the elevator at school? What about the Christmas pageant back in Baltimore, when all the kids carried lit candles? We visited their graves every summer when we visited my grandparents in Pennsylvania.

There were also questions. There were also questions that went unspoken—or at least I don't remember asking anyone. If I did, the answers weren't satisfactory. I'm one of those people who will keep asking until someone gives me an answer that at least makes sense to me. Looking back, every one of those losses reinforced that broken trust. It was another reason not to feel safe, another reason not to love, another reason to not believe in God's love and mercy, another reason to feel abandoned and listen to the voices in my head that each loss was my fault, and another reason to hide and find comfort in that dish of ice cream or candy bar.

My life was shaped by that lack of trust and the litany of reasons why I was right not to trust, but I never saw it. No one shined a light and said, "Don't believe the voices. Don't listen." So, I put one foot in front of the other and did what I was supposed to do. Yet, there was always a nagging feeling that something was missing or wrong.

My life was moving along quite well. I used to say that everything fell apart when I lost my job, or maybe when my Mom almost died one Christmas. Yup, looking at losses again, and once again I did what I thought was expected of me. And, things were about to change in such I way that I couldn't help but reach out.

Let me begin this part in May 2000. At one level I was living an ideal life — I shared a beautiful townhouse in the Virginia suburbs of D.C. with my mother and oldest niece who was just finishing her first year of teaching. I had three special cats, a cadre of friends and my sister was graduating from the Lutheran Theological Seminary at Gettysburg.

Days before graduation, a routine doctor's visit turned into yet another hospital stay for Mom. Nothing all that unusual. Mom's health was fragile ever since she moved in with me more than three years before. Graduation went off without a hitch. I expected Mom to come home after they had her stabilized. I didn't expect the news her doctors delivered that Monday morning — Mom had two to four months to live.

I knew that every day during the past three and a half years had been a gift, and yet the prognosis was startling. Loss was not new, but this was different. I consciously felt responsible for keeping things together this time — responsible for keeping my Mom alive. Yes, this is not logical or rational. But it wasn't a logical or rational equation. It was colored with many losses and other childhood trauma, with unanswered questions and the guilt of a small child.

### What is one to do when facing a parent's death?

Reaching out to friends for prayers felt like a great first step, so I e-mailed everyone I knew to ask for prayers for Mom during this transition time. I never thought to ask for prayers for me. Greg, an acupuncturist whom I had seen for a brief period the year before, graciously offered to include Mom's spirit in the Sufi healing circle he participated in.

I was collapsing both physically and emotionally as I faced losing not only a parent but also my best friend. It meant losing someone who had loved me, cared for me, and nurtured me my entire life. At the same time, I was watching the collapse of a strong, capable and giving woman who had faced the world alone after losing her husband of 25 years and her 16-year-old daughter within three months of each other. She was a woman who had raised five children and faced the challenges of watching her daughter fight polio from the age of three months. She came from hearty stock. Her mother was an impressive, substantial woman and yet loving and giving at the same time. Her father gave so much and really never stopped working until he was diagnosed with lung cancer. Here she was barely 100 pounds, needing oxygen 24/7 and finally requiring a feeding tube and not ready to give up the fight. Enter Sufism, stage right.

I was not ready to give up the fight either. I saw my Mom going downhill, but I wasn't ready to say goodbye. The thread of healing, light and hope came through Greg's kind offer.

Touched by his offer, I recalled a technique he had taught me years before called Remembrance and the peace it seemed to bring when I did it during our appointments. As I understood it, all you needed to do was repeat a name for God. Greg's teacher, Dr. Ibrahim Jaffe, explained that using a sacred language made the technique more powerful. I didn't understand anything about sacred language and wasn't willing to use the name Allah, which had been suggested by Dr. Jaffe.

I settled on Yahweh, which being Hebrew seemed more sacred than saying God. Somehow repeating the word God over and over again seemed silly, but using the Hebrew word made it feel like I was actually calling on God to help. I don't know who I was trying to help during these times when I would do Remembrance. I do recall being scared. Mom was in the ICU, while I was in the hospital waiting room and grabbing at anything I thought could make a difference.

In June, I suffered my first bout of acute bronchitis and yet was making daily visits to the hospital or nursing home. As hard as this was for me physically and emotionally, I am glad I did it. I was blessed to be working with an amazing therapist. She helped me to see the gift that I was being offered and to be available for my Mom. Thea's insight continues to bear fruit and helps me to look beyond and to receive the blessings that are being offered.

My Mom passed in early July.

## The Aftermath of Loss: The Open Doorway.

My health went downhill. I had a few more bouts of acute bronchitis and I suffered from depression. The blessings and gifts were there, if I looked beyond the losses, illnesses, trauma and more. Sufism continues to help me find those blessings and gifts and to shift my perspective.

After my third bout of acute bronchitis within eight months, I reached out to Greg again for some help. You could say that this third episode is when I finally walked through the open doorway with tentative first steps. Each step was cautious, and I needed to navigate around any trust landmines. I was fortunate to be surrounded by gentle, caring and sensitive souls who allowed me to find safety at each step rather than pushing me.

While my steps were cautious and tentative, I was also desperately seeking emotional peace and physical healing. I jumped right into weekly appointments (or more) with Greg and started attending some Sufi gatherings, including the healing circles that Greg had told me about. I was so thirsty that I said yes to almost every one of the Sufi events that I heard about. There were still questions holding me back. I just didn't feel safe enough yet to take the next big step – officially becoming a student of this man they called Sidi.

One day, seemingly out of the blue, it felt right, and I said yes. Looking back on that day, I can see how I had been testing, exploring and looking for safety from the moment I started attending Sufi events. The conscious questions centered on the Sufi teachings—how the teachings differed from the Lutheran teachings I had grown up with, and about the impact on my family in this world and the next. The subconscious questions focused on building trust and feeling safe—could I trust these people? Were these teachings going to take me away from the people and beliefs that helped me feel safe?

I can't say that all my questions were answered by the time I said yes, but enough safety and trust had been developed that I felt comfortable enough to jump in. And, jump in I did. From a short weekend workshop, I jumped into a 2-week long trip to California. My time in California was split between a week-long Sufi camp in rural Northern California, and the second week was at a Sufi healing retreat in Santa Rosa. I returned home to attend another weekend workshop and to sign up for Sufi healing school, which has now become USHS. I kept swimming in the deep end with even more workshops and other activities.

Even with all that swimming in the deep end, the core of my trust issues stayed hidden. You could say that I didn't feel safe enough yet to face them.

Fast forward a couple of years and circumstances had once again put me at a crossroads: my job at the natural food store was ending, as was my one-week stint at the fireworks store. I was moving off the farm where I had lived for the past year. I was once again being given a chance to find the core and uncover some buried treasure. I had decided to volunteer at the Sufi retreat center in Northern California for four weeks. This month would be a working retreat for me. During the week, I would work in the office and weekends would give me the retreat time that my spirit was craving.

About three weeks into my stay, I shared my weekend retreat with two women. The weekend daily schedule was simple—check-ins, reading and writing Sidi's books and remembering. While the outer form changes, all of our practices are about remembering—dusting off our connection to our Creator and remembering who we were created to be.

The check-ins that weekend were unremarkable and yet profound at the deepest level. I walked away from the Saturday morning check-in, thinking how Allah works in strange and mysterious ways. I was clearly seeing how Allah puts in front of us those circumstances, people, and situations that stir our pots—not intended to harm us or to bring us sadness, but to heal us and bring us home. I didn't see that He was doing the same for me. I only saw what He was doing for these two women. You know, the forest and the trees.

We had an expression in healing school—it's like peeling an onion. You take away the first layer to reveal the deeper layers remaining untouched. With many of the Sufi metaphors, the depth of meaning ends only when you have finished exploring. I was being set up to discover the buried treasure from so long ago—each weekend had taken me to a new layer of the onion, enabling me to dive a little bit deeper into the depths of who I am. With no warning, I was handed a hunk of garbage. However, I knew that hidden inside was a treasure so precious that it would forever change me and my relationship with the world, but more importantly my relationship with God.

Waking up from a nap, I touched on the first conscious memories of that long ago childhood trauma and began to understand the core of the trust issues, even if I couldn't name them yet. A couple of years later, I could finally name that core issue after that fateful conversation in the car. I am so grateful to those two sisters and the teachers that guided me during those weekends in retreat.

It wasn't until I started facing the childhood trauma, that I could truly start rebuilding the trust and begin to know who I was created to be. I am still learning all these years later. The beauty that I've uncovered within and without have been a priceless gift.

## Carol Maryam Reimer, M.S.T.

Maryam Reimer is our Development Director at USHS. She strives to create open doors and sustaining relationships supporting all to drink from the deeply sacred teachings offered by the University as they travel their own unique journey to Divine Love, Mercy and Peace.

Maryam's path to Sufism came through loss of beloved family members and childhood trauma. In her search for a way out of depression and to wholeness, she found Sufism and the doorstep of Shaykh Sidi Muhammad al Jamal.

Maryam has worked in the zawiyyahs (retreats) at the Farm of Peace in Pennsylvania and the Shadhiliyya Sufi Center in California. She also holds a B.S. in Accounting from St. John Fisher College and an M.S. in Taxation from DePaul University.

# Self-Acceptance

## Amany Shalaby, M.A., Sidi's Interpreter

I remember a particular incident when I was around four years old which played a role in increasing my fears, self-rejection and feeling of alienation. One day, my mother took me to our neighbor, whose grandmother was visiting and handed me to them. I had no idea that there was a plan to pierce my ears. In those days, it was done in a primitive way. I was held tightly and sensed danger and then felt the shocking pain of piercing my ears. Of course, I screamed loudly and was terrified. Later my mother held me and they took me to look at the mirror and pointed to my earring: "Look how beautiful your earrings are! All girls must have earrings and now you have one like all the girls." I never visited that neighbor, without checking if the grandmother was there.

When I look back at this incident, I believe that in a very subtle and deep way, it made me associate being a girl and being feminine with having to experience pain. My sense of self-rejection unconsciously started at that time. For many years, I wished that I was a boy. This was because boys had easier roles in society and they did not get their ears pierced. I started to reject wearing very feminine clothes but I was not always successful. My mother always had the last word. I also grew to hate makeup and ornaments. This had made me feel different from other girls. My mother's comments comparing me with other girls, in order to encourage me to try these things, made me feel that I did not fit in girlhood. She had also decided to cut my hair short to be easy to care for. This made me the subject of some bullying at elementary school. I can now see how I was growing in self-rejection and asking why God created me as a girl.

There was something else that made me feel insecure as a young woman. It was sexual harassment in the Egyptian streets, which unfortunately was a common practice. I used to walk about forty-five minutes to my high school. Along the way, I heard lewd verbal comments and whistles, which many women across the world still experience today. I remember one day in particular when I felt really angry and scared. A man had followed me for fifteen minutes until I arrived at school. He made lewd comments about my body and for the first time I eventually yelled at a man to stop. Once I saw my friends, I burst into tears and told them how I felt scared and insulted. I felt my body was violated and that I hated being a girl, because it meant I had to be subjected to that.

This sense of self-rejection and insecurity continued during my marriage and was intensified with many incidents, like when my husband asked me to put on makeup, criticized my looks or asked me to change my hair style. When my husband insisted that I should pierce my ears and wear earrings, all the pain and fear came to the surface. It was as if Allah wanted to bring it out, so I could become aware of these unconscious memories and release them. When I look back at my experiences, I could see how my ex-husband, who lost his father at a young age and his mother when he was in middle school, had carried his pain and insecurities from his childhood experiences. This was also reflected in our relationships. However, both of us were unconscious of it at the time or were too afraid and unwilling to face our insecurities and sadness. We were projecting them onto one another and in our lives in general in one way or another. Our problems eventually led to divorce.

I was at my lowest moment with low self-esteem and a broken heart. At that time, I'd been introduced to the Sufi path through reading the poetry of a Sufi woman who later became my friend and therapist. She manifested confidence, self-acceptance and ecstasy in the way she described her love for Allah. I wanted to have a similar experience. I immersed myself in dhikr for many days, weeks or even months, in making art and crafts with no sense of what should be my next step or which direction should I take. I found great comfort and healing of my sadness.

Nonetheless, I faced the difficulty of having to support myself with not enough child support. My youngest daughter was two years old. I could not leave her to go back to school or work. I had no family in the US to support me and felt all alone and helpless. In addition, my ex-husband got married. I felt that my heart was crushed and shattered, in spite of the fact that I was the one who initiated the divorce and knew for certain we could not be together again. I was angry and jealous as well as sad and lonely. It intensified because there was no one there for me but Allah. I received a beautiful inspiration to repeat a particular prayer. It was that particular prayer that rescued me from my anguish. I was inspired to repeat: "I am a woman by Allah, from Allah and for Allah." As I repeated the prayers, more insights, beautiful visions and self-acceptance started to pour in.

The inner Garden within me started to open, and its flowers started to bloom outwardly. Inwardly, I started to have spiritual experiences, in which I felt the Divine Presence, gained an understanding of myself and others and got answers to many of my pressing questions. I also started to have visions and guidance of where to go and what to do. I started volunteering to cook for the homeless shelter. Seeing people who were suffering more than me, had helped to heal my own pain. More importantly, I felt loved by Allah. I felt my self-worth as a representative of Allah. I volunteered in many other places and shared in founding a non-profit organization to help single women, even though I was in need of help myself, but only Allah knew about it. I started to look for Sufi teachers and Sufi groups. I knew that I could find healing in Sufi company, wisdom and guidance.

One of the groups I joined on the internet, was moderated by Dr. Allan Godlas. I expressed to him my desire to work in translating Sufi books. One day, I saw myself in a dream holding papers in my hand in which "Palestine" was written. I was wondering why these papers were in my hands. I then saw myself entering a hall. I found a group of people and among them was a friend of mine in real life. Her name is "Shifa" which means "healing." She said, "I found this group of people who heal by the Beautiful Divine Names, especially by two Names" al-Hannan (The Tenderly Loving) and al-Mannan (The Grantor of Gifts)." Behind Shifa, I saw a man who said, "This is another group of the Lovers of Allah." I woke up feeling longing and yearning to see this group. I wanted to be among the lovers who have tender love and are gifted to heal.

A week later, Dr. Godlas called me and asked if I could translate for Sidi, a Shaikh from Jerusalem. My heart jumped with excitement. I needed a job and it was an opportunity to meet another Sufi Shaikh. He put me in contact with Amina al-Jamal, the publisher of Sidi's books. All obstacles seemed to ease and I was set to travel to California with my children to instantly translate for him. I asked how a Shaikh from Jerusalem would know a group of people in California. Amina informed me that it was through the Jaffe institute for spiritual healing by the Names of Allah. I gasped as I remembered the dream and was assured that I would meet a wonderful group. However, I was unsure if I would be able to do the job, since I am not a professional translator. Looking back, I could see how Allah had prepared me for the job. It was not only through my free readings and studies, but also through volunteering to help the Imam in our local mosque whose English was not fluent and who would ask me, as a frequent volunteer in the mosque, to translate his Friday speeches or dialogues with visitors, which I gladly did. I learned from this experience that if you cannot find a job you should volunteer in something you are passionate about. If you need more income, give charity. What goes around comes around because Allah is al-Karim (The Generous) and ash-Shakur (The Thankful).

But in spite of what I gained from my volunteer translation and readings, I was still insecure in my ability to simultaneously translate for the Imam of al-Masjid al-Aqsaa as he spoke to an American gathering. Therefore, when I arrived in California, I asked Wadude to help arrange a meeting for me and Sidi before the lecture started. This would allow me to ask him to speak slowly. Wadude said that when he asked Sidi to meet me, Sidi remained silent. I was baffled and worried. However, Wadude assured me that everything would be fine. I anxiously waited for Sidi to arrive at the door of the lecture hall. As he arrived, Wadude introduced me. Sidi looked at me and said, "You are my daughter." At first, I took it as one of the common Arab courteous expressions. But Sidi looked deep into my eyes and said in a firm assuring voice, "You are my daughter. From now on, I am your father. I will care for you." I felt a sense of security shower over me. We entered the hall and he started his regular chanting. I felt at a loss. Should I start translating now or would he instruct me when it was time to start? It was too late to start anyway, so I remained silent until he finished the chanting and started to address his audience. I started to translate his sentence, as he was uttering the following sentence. I did not fully know how I was going to translate the next one. It felt like I was thrown into an ocean where there is one wave coming after the other. I had to surf the waves and go high with the high wave and low with a low wave. I had to be one with the ocean. The words were flowing. I was drowning in their deep meanings and emerging out of the water to breathe them out to people. I forgot myself, and my anxiousness, fears, and insecurities were gone. I got out of myself. I cried when words moved me and rejoiced when words cheered me. I felt love spelling out of me to the audience, since I wanted them to understand the Path that helped me and would help them.

The first lecture was about the status of women, as a reflection of the Divine Beauty manifesting through women and the true meaning of sacred femininity and sexuality. Sidi later invited me and my children to join him at lunch. This is when we got to chat. He did not ask me many questions about my life. However, from the way he spoke to me, I felt that he fully understood me. He said he chose this particular lecture for me. Tears streamed from my eyes because I knew it. I felt his deep compassion and acceptance. I felt valued and found my role to serve a higher goal than myself. I started to experience the deep understanding of femininity as a representation of the Divine. It is sacred and cherished by Allah and sacred sexuality has deep understanding that is related to our spiritual growth and realization. I started not only to accept myself as a woman but started to love being a woman in the holy way, especially with Sidi's assurance, sincere and loving words. He told me, "You are a complete woman in Allah's Eyes." His words affirmed my inspiration. He assured me that I had not made any mistakes. He said that Allah knew what I went through and why I did or did not do things and that Allah is All-Forgiving. During this whole year, he continued to lecture about the spiritual status of women and how they must be respected and treated with gentleness as sacred beings. The more he taught, the more I felt healed.

I was happy, yet I was afraid to fully accept my happiness and receive the Divine Love from Sidi and from the community. I realized that fear during a spiritual healing that was offered to me by Salih Cotten. During the healing, I started to weep, and as I looked deeper, I realized that I was afraid to accept love and happiness because I was afraid to lose them later. Salih told me a few words, which still ring in my ears today. He said, "No. You would not ever lose this type of love and this type of acceptance and joy, because this is different from worldly love. It is from Allah." Yes, my life experience proved to me that this type of love and joy in Allah is indestructible. Its effects stay within you and come to aid you in difficult times.

From that day on, Sidi acted as a father to me. On the emotional level, Sidi taught me to be self-confident and to accept myself. During one intense experience of dhikr, I saw a vision: I saw myself when I was little girl, crying and afraid. I could literally hear that little girl crying, as if she were another person living inside me. Sidi taught me to embrace this girl, comfort her and let her go. He guided me to forgive my mother, as I started to see that we all go through similar experiences in our childhood that project into our relationships with others.

Sidi taught me the way out and to let go of these past memories. He guided me to be authentic to myself and not to be afraid to address my needs, my feelings, my fears and my thoughts in a polite way. I also learned not to be afraid to speak truth to power and to stand for myself or on behalf of another, and to stand up for women and their rights. He taught me to trust Allah and empowered me to be strong. He taught me not by his words, but mostly by his actions, by the practices he taught us and as I observed him giving advice to countless people who would come to him for counseling.

## Amany Shalaby, M.A., Sidi's Interpreter

Amany Shalaby, M.A., is a poet, author and teacher of Islam and Sufi studies. She works as a translator of Islamic books and teaches in diverse study circles across the states on Islamic spirituality. Amany is the author of *The Essence of Creation, The Emanation of Consciousness* and her book of poetry, *Hidden Pearls.* Amany served as Sidi's interpreter for twelve years.

Amany graduated as an electrical engineer from `Ein Shams University, Cairo, Egypt in 1985. She obtained her Post Graduate Diploma in Islamic Studies from Islamic College of Advancing Studies, Middlesex University, London, UK in 2002 and her Master's degree in Comparative Philosophy of Religions in 2014 from the Islamic College of Advancing Studies, Middlesex University, London, UK.

She is on the faculty of The University of Spiritual Healing & Sufism. She is a co-founder of Radiant Hands Inc., an organization that helps single mothers in need.

# *Everywhere you turn is the face of Allah*

# Salima Maxine Adelstein, M.Ed., D.D.

I have often wondered, what am I doing here, what is the point, why is there so much sadness and misery in the world? Can I ever find peace and truth and happiness?

This was not a prayer, just a nagging question in my soul that even 20 years of meditation provided no clear answers. Then a wise man said do not ask "why or what" and was able to answer each of these questions and take me on the most exquisite journey of my life so far.

I have always been a seeker and traveler for Truth. This latest adventure started in Egypt traveling down the Nile, hearing a call that moved the depth of my soul. I did not understand what it was at the time, but the melody touched my heart and opened a space to explore the stirrings of my soul. We have moments in our life that define what is important and what is meaningful. That was one of those moments. It was years before I discovered exactly how significant that moment in time was. It was like a tapestry where each thread apparently seems like an independent entity. However, if you weave them together, the picture becomes clear and beautiful. It becomes the tapestry of your life and an expression of who and what you have done that all gets woven together into your legacy. It involves your contributions to the world and the way and ways that you make a difference.

Each of us has a unique tapestry. It is a God-given talent that gets expressed in this life and will call upon us in the next life. To gain a glimpse of my tapestry and to be able to open that door to others, has been the fulfillment of my deepest desires to be of service, help, guide, and support others in times of happiness and sadness. It involves joy and disappointment as well as life and death.

I grew up by the ocean. Staring at the endless horizon always gave me pause for reflection and wonder at what lies beneath the vast ocean. I had the opportunity to learn to scuba dive. There, I experienced a sense of wonder and awe at the oneness with all that is around you. They call it neutral buoyancy. It is a sense of floating in the water, rather than being bounced around on top of the surface with the waves that are often tumultuous, but the bottom of the ocean floor beneath the surface is calm and all is peace and all is one.

Years later, I again experienced this unity. It was not a fleeting experience but a station of the journey home. The difference between a state and a station is one is passing, while the other is abiding.

In order to abide in this station of unity, all of my separations, illusions needed to be explored, experienced and enveloped into a metamorphosis of love, peace and mercy.

My intention was to find someone who could help, support and guide me there. I wound up in Jerusalem to study with Sidi al Jamal, the Head of the higher council for Jerusalem and the Holy Land.

I met Sidi in the States, but was not attracted to the Sufi Path. I was a meditator and loved my meditation practices. I was not looking for a new path. However, my heart was yearning, knowing that there was something more. I trusted my heart's knowing and opened the door to a new chapter that would change my life forever.

It did require a letting go. It meant letting go of my work, home, family, friends and all that I thought I knew, and emptying myself to learn something new.

There is an old Sufi saying: "If you come to a guide with a thimble, he will fill it with a thimbleful of water, and if you come with a bucket, he will fill the bucket."

There is a beautiful story of the founder of the Shadhuliyya Sufis that best illustrates this. Hasan ash-Shadhuli was a seeker of Truth. At the age of twenty fine, he travelled to the East searching for a master who possessed the complete knowledge and was known as the Pole of his time. He studied with some of the great masters and eventually was led to Mashish, who lived right at the base of the mountain where he grew up. Each time he ascended the mountain, he was told to return and do wudu (the ritual washing of the body before prayer). This happened three times before he finally understood that he needed to not only wash his body, but wash away all that he had learned to come to his master with an empty heart ready to be filled with Divine knowledge. When he realized this and again did wudu, this time Mashish met him half way and embraced and welcomed him as a student.

I thought I was ready to be filled with Divine knowledge, but it was not so. I was still full of "I know." As a result, my time in Jerusalem was anything but easy. It challenged everything that I thought I knew and believed to be true. However, studying with Sidi in his zawiyah in Jerusalem was the answer to all those questions I had and set the spiritual direction of my next journey.

His loving presence reminded me of a time on the beach, when I was struggling with life's inequalities and injustices. I "met" Jesus, who told me that I was a healer (another story and another time). Sidi set up a healing space for me to work. I felt like he saw me and deeply knew who I was, no matter what I did, where I wandered and how lost I was. He was always there, reminding me of who I was and what the Truth was and what was illusion.

Wherever I turned, there was the Face of God or Allah, as I was learning the name for God. God in his paradigm was called Allah and I was still getting used to that name.

Sidi was a Sufi Muslim sheik. His teachings were based in Islam. It was a religion I knew nothing about and having been brought up Jewish, I had been taught that Muslims are not to be trusted and are an enemy to the Jews. As a role model, I was much more attracted to Mother Theresa, and if I had my way would have chosen to study with her.

Wow! Did I have a lot to learn. My heart had so many of what in Sufism are called veils. Veils of light and veils of darkness. So many places of separation and pain. So many places that needed cleaning and purifying. I was lucky to have any space at all left in my heart. No wonder I was drawn to a life of service. Now I was beginning to understand and know. To come out of the understandings in my mind to the deeper wisdom in my heart.

My first night in Jerusalem, I was deeply afraid. Afraid that someone would find out that I was Jewish and try to kill me. I awoke to the sound of loud banging and yelling for me to come quickly. He said to follow him and I was sure this was my death. In Sufism, we say die before you die, but this was not what it felt like. When I arrived where he was taking me, it turned out to be Sidi's son and his mother was sick. He said, "My dad said you are a healer. Can you help her?" I felt very foolish, and at that moment my heart opened to help someone in distress. The room was full of relatives, family and friends. I was used to being alone with someone, not a room full of watchers. However, here I was and that was the situation.

Everything I knew about healing was gone. Any psychic sight or empathic feelings disappeared. All of the tools that I had in my toolbox were not available. I was figuratively deaf and blind and feeling pretty dumb. All I had was the deepest desire to be of service, to surrender and to deeply rely on a power greater that my own to continue. I forgot to mention that she spoke Arabic and no English. I spoke English and no Arabic. Therefore, we did not have any verbal way of communicating during the healing.

My hands did what my hands do in a healing. After some time she sat up, smiled and said "Alhumdulillah." I then realized that the healing was over and her family and friends surrounded her with hugs and kisses. I learned my first words of Arabic that day, "alhumdulillah." It means all thanks and praises are from Allah (God).

When I left the room, Sidi was reclining on his mat. He smiled up at me. It reminded me of the first of many lessons that I would learn in this retreat. "Everywhere you turn, there is the Face of Allah." God's compassion and mercy is in everything and in every situation. Allah is the healer. I am nothing, only a servant of God's will. All else is an illusion.

"Everywhere you turn there is the Face of God." God's love, healing, peace, mercy and compassion never leaves us. The Qur'an says Allah is closer to you than your jugular vein. This applies whether you are distant or near, feeling connected or not, and in the flow or not. Experiencing the loving presence or not, God, Allah, is there. In the darkest moments or the brightest revelations, God says, "Remember me and I will remember you. Call upon me and I am here." This teaching is something I come back to again and again. It is a reminder and a remembrance.

Remembrance is one of the foundational practices of the Sufi way. It is both a reminder of who we are in Truth and a remembrance of the longing in our hearts to know yourself and to know God. It washes and purifies the heart so that it becomes a clear mirror reflecting the beauty that lives in each one of us. Sidi writes, "When God created you He created beauty." I had to fight a lot of voices that said, "Yes that is true for others, but not me." Each time I would do the practice of remembrance, voices of "not good enough," "this applies to others, not me," and "I may be cute but not beautiful" were popping up in my consciousness. Each time I practiced the remembrance, it slowly starting clearing the path to see the beauty, to wash away the falsehoods, and to experience some peace and calm inside me. The best way I can describe it is like a big hug of Love that surrounded the voices and absorbed them in this ocean of Love, so there was only Love and Peace.

No matter how much I struggled or resisted, Sidi was a constant reminder of that Love and peace and compassion. Each assignment he gave me opened up new doors to understanding and melted any resistance I was holding. When he asked me to learn the five daily prayers Muslim do, I had my biggest rebellion. I know how to pray and I have been praying all of my life. Why did I need to learn some foreign prayers? He himself said, "Make no difference or separation." Wasn't this a separation and difference?

So, I went on an adventure. I left the zawiyah and ventured out into the sacred precinct in Jerusalem where Muslims, Jews and Christians all have holy sites. My first stop was at the Wailing Wall. I had visited there many years ago with my family and knew the ritual. I stood at the wall and prayed and left a note of peace in the wall. A beautiful feeling of the presence of God came over me. It was soft and feminine and full of beauty and peace. The fact that it was the prayers I knew from childhood and loved most likely helped.

The next stop was at the Church and a visit to Jesus's tomb. Normally, there are lots of people there. However, on this day there were no lines. I took it as a sign that I was doing the right thing and went in to sit in the tomb. I got on my knees, prayed, felt a loving presence and asked to help to understand why we all pray differently. The same loving presence I felt as a teenager on a walk on the beach when I believed Jesus said to me, "You are a healer," was a reminder of the Love that Jesus brought to this world. This was both comforting and reassuring to my spirit, but it was not an answer to my question.

I then went to the Dome of the Rock and the al-Aqsa mosque. In Sufism, we have voices to discern and also pictures. My pictures were that this is not my place. This was very different and strange. I felt my mother's disapproval and felt a betrayal of my roots. Nevertheless I entered, since I was on a mission to somehow understand and to bring together the beauty of these monotheistic religions.

I again heard the call to prayer. My heart was again moved, as it was that day on the Nile. I watched and followed the ladies do the movements of standing, bending, kneeling and prostrating. In each movement, I felt the coming together of each of the prophets, Abraham, Moses, Jesus and Mohammad. I felt a washing of my light body and the angels singing God's praises. Tears started pouring from my eyes and I felt that "everywhere you turn there is the face of God." I wanted to return to the zawiyah to tell Sidi about my experience.

When I returned to the zawiyah, I expected Sidi to be upset that I left. My zawiyah mom, Maryam, was. She could not understand why I wanted to leave the safety of the zawiyah and go out into the world. When Sidi came in, he knew where I had gone, and instead of congratulating me, he said, "Why do you make difference and separation?"

At that moment, I experienced in my heart a wall that started to come down brick by brick. Each picture was shattered by love, and I got a glimpse of the jewel in my heart. I started crying again as Sidi put his hand in my hand and asked me to say "la ilaha ila llah, Muhammadan rasulullah." He said, "These are holy tears, remembering all the time I wasted." At that moment, my whole being was in surrender to the ONE and I knew I was a Muslim. I was one who surrenders herself to God's will.

Learning the five times-a-day prayers took on new meaning and intention. It was a blessing and an opportunity to wash all the dirt I accumulated during the day. It was an opportunity to clean and feel refreshed and lighter. It was an opportunity to talk to God.

When Sidi asked me to pray for something I wanted, I was confused and bewildered. Doesn't God know what I want? Why did I need to pray for something that the Lord knows already? What I realized is that I was learning to care for myself. I was learning to ask for what I need and to let my voice be heard. It was an important lesson for me. When I am tired or feeling fatigue, it helps to be reminded to pray for what you need. God is the Provider and fulfills our needs. Then I turn towards God instead of others. It gives me the strength and the nourishment that I need to be in the world with all its ups and downs.

I continued my studies in the zawiyah and gained new insights and revelations about myself. Gnostic understanding of some of those deep questions in my life were revealing themselves to me. I was feeling whole and complete. Sidi's guidance was like a lighthouse shining the way into the home of God in my heart. He asked me to stare at the name Allah in Arabic for hours. He showed me a book that had a cross section of the heart where the name Allah in Arabic is written. When I stared at the name like that, I was enlivening the name within my heart like seeds that grow into beautiful flowers.

Many secrets and hidden treasures are hidden in the heart, waiting for us to wake up and explore. He writes, "You think you are a small star, when in fact you comprise the entire universe." When I felt like I was depending on Sidi, he constantly reminded me:

*This way is not like any other Sufi way. It is to be special only for God. There is no shaykh in this way—there is only Allah. Through the spirit which is linked without beginning and without end, to the spirits of the prophets, the one who truly follows and obeys from the Reality can find herself inside the real garden of the heart of the Beloved.*

Look for the signs of God in creation. They are everywhere, because wherever you turn, there is the face of God, Allah. Compassion, Mercy, Love, Peace, Freedom and Beauty and on and on. The ending is just the beginning. Love and Love and Love...

I would like to share a poem Sidi wrote that sums up my time in zawiyah with him:

*You are He, He is you His love is your love.*
*When you give everything for yourself without why or what*
*And you come to be in His garden,*
*When you taste the sweetness through His reality,*
*When you finish with everything not for Him,*
*how can I say "for Him?"*
*There is nothing, only He.*
*My holy beloved, my holy child*
*Who I am waiting for,*

*If you know Who is calling you*
*To be between His arms.*

*And why He is calling you,*
*Because you carry His jewel.*
*You carry Him and you have everything from Him for Him.*
*Really, you are the life and you have the wine of His life.*
*You have the fire to destroy everything not for Him.*
*But be ready always and move your tongue with His name.*
*Be careful not to look back*
*Or to say "why" or "what"*
*But trust and surrender and throw yourself before His door.*
*I mean about His door, the door of His love.*
*You are His love, nothing else can carry Him*
*He is inside you; and contains you, as you contain Him.*
*For this holy world He makes you His image; to be hidden;*
*And He is waiting for you to return from whence you came.*
*You know through His word you can throw yourself inside the station of His*
*word.*
*La ilaha ila 'llah Muhammadan rasulullah.*

# Salima Maxine Adelstein, M.Ed., D.D.

Salima Maxine Adelstein has been a spiritual leader, teacher and healer for the past 30 years. She studied extensively in Jerusalem and Morocco with the leading Sufi masters of our time, including Sidi Muhammad al-Jamal, head of the Higher Sufi Council in the Holy Land and Jerusalem and Iman at the Al-Aqsa mosque, who gave her the rank of Murshid (spiritual guide) of the Shadhuliyya Sufi Order.

She is a Co-founder and Co-President of The University of Spiritual Healing and Sufism and the Academic Dean and Department Head of the Spiritual Ministry and Sufi Studies Master's Program. Salima founded the Farm of Peace, The International Peace Center and Sufi Center East community in the Mid-Atlantic region of the United States.

Salima has been invited to speak at a variety of conferences in the United States, Mexico and England. Her lectures combine both experiential and didactic methods to engage participants' minds and hearts in the exploration of Truth, Peace, Freedom, Justice, Love and Compassion.

Salima combines stories, a sense of humor and a deep connection to the Divine, helping each individual find the happiness and truth of their own beings.

# Closing

Our guide, Sidi Muhammad al-Jamal, left his physical body on November 11, 2015. Before he left, he assured us that he had given us everything we need to carry on his mission of spreading the message of peace, love, mercy, justice and freedom in the world.

The University of Spiritual Healing and Sufism was established in 2006 to teach spiritual healing and transformation. Our programs teach students how to heal themselves and others, and how to move from living a life of ego to living a life of the soul and beyond.

Each of the authors in this book works with the University to teach healing, peacemaking, ministry and spiritual leadership to people who are seeking to discover their unique gifts and serve the world in a Divinely-guided way.

Since Sidi's passing, God has continued to call people to this path and to the University. The door is open for all to join us in continuing this mission. There is much work to be done in this world.

If you are called to join us, to discover how your unique talents and gifts can be used to serve and make a difference in the world, we invite you to visit our website and consider joining us for one of our programs.

We offer a variety of online programs, distance learning courses and in-person events. Our flagship program is the Masters of Divinity, with specialties in Advanced Spiritual Healing of Disease, Spiritual Ministry & Sufi Studies, and Spiritual Peacemaking.

You can find out more about the University and our programs at our website:

http://SufiUniversity.org

email: outreach@sufiuniversity.org

PO Box 729

Angwin, CA 94508

Phone: 800.238.3060

# Prayer from Sidi for America and all of the World

My Lord, I ask You to keep all of my beloveds in this way. I ask You to keep Your door always open for everyone who comes to You searching for the Truth. I ask You to heal everyone who is sick - to heal him and to use him in the right way.

I ask You to send the peace, love, mercy, justice and freedom everywhere, to all the people in this world. I ask You to give the people who live in America the real peace, the real love and the real freedom. I ask You to protect every child here from every bad thing. And to heal everyone who is crying and who is hungry, and to send Your flag, the flag of unity, the flag of love to this country.

Help the people who live here, and Europe and Africa and everywhere, to live with each other and to help each other. Help them to hear Your voice, the song of the peace and the love. Help us always to see the flag of unity in every home and to sing this holy song. Amin.

Made in the USA
San Bernardino, CA
09 August 2017